22 DAYS IN FLORIDA

THE ITINERARY PLANNER

RICHARD HARRIS
WITH TAMALYN HARRIS

John Muir Publications
Santa Fe, New Mexico

Thanks to Tom Bellucci, Julian Cordero, Laura Craig, Carl and
Ruth Harris, Mary Hartsfield, Joanna Hill, Jeanne Hinchcliff,
Pete and Evelyn Lujan, Kaaren Mils, Richard Polese, Mary
Shapiro, and Michael and Mara Taylor for helping make this
book possible. Very special thanks to Rita Guidi, who braved
mosquitoes, traffic jams, predawn canoe journeys, and a Florida
snowstorm in search of the state's natural areas and Native
American heritage.

John Muir Publications, P.O. Box 613, Santa Fe, NM 87504

First edition. Second printing

Library of Congress Cataloging-in-Publication Data
Harris, Richard, 1947-
    22 days in Florida: the itinerary planner/Richard Harris
with Tamalyn Harris.— 1st ed.
    p.   cm.
    ISBN 0-945465-27-0
    1. Florida—Description and travel—1981 - —Tours. I. Harris,
Tamalyn. II. Title. III. Title: Twenty-two days in Florida.
F309.3.H3   1989
917.5904'43—dc20   89-12926
                                                          CIP

Distributed to the book trade by:
W.W. Norton & Company, Inc.
New York, New York

Design   Mary Shapiro
Maps   Michael Taylor
Cover   Jim Wood
Typography   Copygraphics, Santa Fe, NM

CONTENTS

PENSACOLA

ALA.

GEORGIA

TALLAHASSEE

JACKSONVILLE

ST. AUGUSTINE

Atlantic Ocean

Gulf of Mexico

CEDAR KEY

OCALA

DAYTONA BEACH

ORLANDO

CAPE CANAVERAL

TAMPA

SARASOTA

WEST PALM BEACH

FORT MYERS

MIAMI

Everglades National Park

KEY LARGO

Florida Keys

KEY WEST

HOW TO USE THIS BOOK

On a bleak autumn day as gray clouds gather on a chill wind and you feel a pang of envy for the birds in their southbound flocks, read this book. Think about January. Think about galoshes in the slush, cars that won't start, windshields caked with ice. Then think about escaping all that. *22 Days in Florida* tells how.

Birds do it—and so can you. This winter, you can wriggle your toes in beach sand, wear hardly any clothes, and return with a golden tan that folks back home will envy. Of course, escaping to Florida for the winter is not a new idea. Thomas Edison thought of it, as did John D. Rockefeller, Ernest Hemingway, Al Capone, and Mickey Mouse, all of whom you'll encounter—in spirit, at least—as you follow the itinerary described in this book.

The itinerary is divided into 22 daily sections, containing:
1. A **suggested schedule** for each day's travel and sightseeing.
2. A detailed **travel route** for each driving segment of your trip.
3. **Sightseeing highlights** (rated in order of importance: ▲▲▲ Don't miss; ▲▲ Try hard to see; and ▲ See if you get a chance).
4. Selective **food, lodging**, and **camping** recommendations.
5. **Helpful hints** and **insights**—random tidbits that will enhance your trip.
6. User-friendly **maps** designed to show you what the road up ahead is really like.

For readers who have less than three weeks to explore Florida, this itinerary divides into one-week segments that can be used independently as excursions from the Orlando, Miami, and Tampa Bay areas.

The first week covers the Atlantic Coast from St. Augustine to Miami. Here you'll find all of Florida's most popular tourist destinations, including Walt Disney World, Daytona Beach, Kennedy Space Center, and Palm Beach, famous places that are well worth the crowds and relatively high prices you'll encounter there.

The second week covers the Miami area and three other south Florida destinations—the Keys, Everglades National Park, and Big Cypress Swamp. These aren't the sort of places you can experience through a windshield, so our suggestions include such activities as snorkeling, canoeing, bicycling, and plenty of walking.

The third week covers the Gulf Coast and takes you to places that relatively few Florida visitors see. There are unique old

homes like Thomas Edison's and John Ringling's and offbeat
museums exhibiting everything from electric trains to bizarre
paintings. You'll also find remote island hideaways, ancient
Indian ceremonial mounds, and, hidden in the forests, crystal-
clear springs.

When to Go

Peak tourist season in most parts of Florida runs from the
Christmas holidays through March. The prices and hours
quoted in this book assume that you'll be traveling during the
winter months. At that time of year, north Florida can be too
chilly to camp comfortably, but more often you'll find it warm,
sunny, and uncrowded. The winter dry season is by far the best
time to visit south Florida.

A Florida visit can be pleasant in late autumn or late spring,
and accommodation rates are lower—sometimes much lower.
The only drawback to taking your trip then is that you won't be
able to phone home and hear about the icicles and subzero tem-
peratures you're missing.

The only really bad time to visit Florida is in the summer
months. Walt Disney World is popular then, but no place else is.
The off-season is known in Everglades National Park as the
"wet season" (a masterpiece of understatement) and in Miami as
the "mean season," a time of violent thunderstorms and big
black clouds of hungry mosquitoes. Hurricanes can happen in
July, August, or September. On the average, a truly mighty hurricane strikes south Florida once every 40 to 50 years. The last big
one, which blew a locomotive into the ocean along the Florida
Keys and stripped the Everglades National Park coast bare of
mangroves, was in 1935. The next one is now overdue.

Lodging

Using the addresses and phone numbers in this book, you can
make room reservations for every night of your trip—and
thereby tie your vacation into a straitjacket with no room for
spontaneity. Don't do it. Lodging reservations almost always
mean putting down a cash or credit card deposit, which you'll
forfeit if you change your travel plan en route. Instead, stay flexi-
ble by only making reservations at a few special places where
they are essential, leaving uncommitted days in between.

You must make reservations months in advance if you plan to
stay at any hotel in Walt Disney World (Days 3 through 5),
Flamingo Lodge in Everglades National Park (Days 12 and 13), or
Wakulla Springs Lodge (Day 21).

You should make reservations at least several weeks in
advance if you plan to stay in any of the luxury beach resorts
mentioned in this book or in bed and breakfasts such as those

suggested for St. Augustine (Day 1) and Key West (Days 10 and 11). In fact, don't even think about driving to Key West without a prearranged place to sleep; if you find yourself without a room there, it's a long drive back.

Reservations are convenient, though not essential, in Miami Beach (Days 7 through 9). Since the Art Deco hotels there are the main sightseeing highlights, there's something to be said for strolling around until you find a vacancy. However, it's much safer to reserve a room for at least the first night so you can store your valuables there instead of leaving them in your vehicle.

Finally, you'll need reservations if you plan to visit Daytona Beach during Speed Weeks (early and mid-February) or spring break (mid-March).

Camping

To surround yourself with natural beauty, your best bet is usually a state park. The Florida Department of Natural Resources provides camping facilities at forty-two parks and recreation areas statewide, and wherever in Florida you happen to find yourself, one of them is likely to be nearby. The avowed purpose of Florida's state park system is to preserve unique natural environments as they were before the first Europeans arrived, so camping in one of these parks usually means a lush forest setting as well as dusk or dawn opportunities to see wildlife. Fees for full-hookup campsites are typically $15 for Florida residents and $18.50 for out-of-staters; some inland parks charge less, while parks in the Florida Keys cost more, and fees seem to change constantly. It often costs less to stay in a private RV park than in a state park, but the state's higher camping fee (which includes admission to the park) is more than justified by the chance to spend a night in one of "real" Florida's little-known, idyllic spots. For information on parks that are not listed in this book, request the free "Florida State Parks Guide" brochure from the Department of Natural Resources, Division of Recreation and Parks, Marjory Stoneman Douglas Building, 3900 Commonwealth Boulevard, Tallahassee, FL 32399.

Some state parks accept campsite reservations, but you'll rarely need them. The only major drawback to state park campgrounds is that no pets are allowed overnight. For those RVers who enjoy animal companionship while traveling, we suggest a nearby privately owned RV park as an alternative to each recommended state park campground. Many of these suggestions are KOA campgrounds, ranging in price from $13 to $30 a night, with small extra charges for more than two people, for air conditioner or heater rental, and sometimes for full hookups. They offer reliable facilities including free showers, cable TV hookups, camp stores, and swimming pools. Kamping Kabins, available at most KOAs, offer weary tent-campers a low-cost indoor alternative for $21 to $35 a night, a rate about midway between the cost of a campsite and the price of a budget motel in the same area. Some KOAs have outstanding settings, such as the Suwanee River (Day 20) and Alligator Point (Day 21). Some have rental boats, hot tubs, restaurants, or other resort features. Purchasing a $6 Kamper Kard the first time you stay at a KOA will save you 10 percent on camping fees beginning the same day you buy it. The card is valid nationwide for two years.

The only private campground listed in this book where reservations are necessary is Fort Wilderness at Walt Disney World (Days 3 through 5).

Campgrounds operated by the federal government, such as those in Everglades National Park (Days 12 and 13) and Ocala National Forest (Days 18 and 19), are among the best bargains you'll find in Florida—$7 a night, first-come, first-served. In Big Cypress National Preserve (Day 14) you can camp for free— no hookups or rest rooms. Pets are allowed in federal campgrounds.

Recommended Reading

We've found most conventional guidebooks to Florida unhelpful. A delightful exception is *The Florida Keys: A History and Guide* by novelist Joy Williams (New York: Random House, 1987), so packed with peculiar tidbits that it would be a pleasure to read even if you weren't planning to visit the Keys.

Miami by Joan Didion (New York: Simon and Schuster, 1987) is not a guidebook. It is a masterpiece of investigative journalism on the politics of Cuban Miami. Anyone who is intrigued by the "capital of Latin America" will be more so after learning about the real rulers of Miami and the roles they've played in recent American history from the Bay of Pigs and the assassination of John Kennedy to the Iran-Contra scandal.

The history of south Florida, from its primeval origins through the mid-twentieth century, is vividly recounted in *The Everglades: River of Grass* by Marjory Stoneman Douglas (St. Simons Island, Ga.: Mockingbird Books), first published in 1947 and still in print, available at the Everglades National Park visitor center and most bookshops in Florida. Also published in inexpensive paperback editions by Mockingbird Books are two classic historical novels about Florida, *The Barefoot Mailman* by Theodore Pratt and *I Take This Land* by Richard Powell. For a catalog of hard-to-find books reissued by this Southern regional paperback publisher, write Mockingbird Cash Sales, P.O. Box 624, St. Simons Island, GA 31522.

The most famous author who ever lived in Florida was Ernest Hemingway. He made his home in Key West for over a decade and wrote several of his best-known works there. The Keys were the setting for two of his novels, *To Have and Have Not* and *Islands in the Stream*. A visit to Hemingway's home may well inspire you to reread any of his books.

The author most fondly remembered by Floridians is not Hemingway but Marjorie Kinnan Rawlings. Her Pulitzer Prize-winning 1938 novel *The Yearling* and her best-selling 1941 memoir *Cross Creek*, both wonderful firsthand accounts of backwoods life in north Florida, are still in print fifty years later. The motion picture version of *Cross Creek* is available on videocassette.

Baseball

One of Florida's top claims to fame is not covered in our main itinerary, but if you're visiting during the month of March, you'll find it everywhere you look. We're talking about spring training. Eighteen American and National League baseball teams warm up for the season and size up the competition in exhibition games every day of the week (totaling more than 500 games in one month) in the Florida Grapefruit League. Practice, which is open to the public, starts at 10:30 a.m. on home game days. Games usually start at 1:00 or 1:30 p.m., 7:30 p.m., or both. Bleacher tickets typically cost $3 or $4, while box seats cost $6 or $7. Here are the Grapefruit League hometowns, the teams that train there, and phone numbers to obtain complete information on schedules and stadium locations:

American League

Boardwalk and Baseball: Kansas City Royals, (800)-367-2249
    from Florida or (800) 826-1939 nationwide
Dunedin: Toronto Blue Jays, (813) 733-9302
Fort Lauderdale: New York Yankees, (305) 776-1921
Lakeland: Detroit Tigers, (813) 682-1401
Miami: Baltimore Orioles, (305) 635-5395
Orlando: Minnesota Twins, (407) 849-6346
Port Charlotte: Texas Rangers, (813) 624-2211
Sarasota: Chicago White Sox, (813) 953-3388
Winter Haven: Boston Red Sox, (813) 293-3900

National League

Bradenton: Pittsburgh Pirates, (813) 748-4610
Clearwater: Philadelphia Phillies, (813) 442-8496
Kissimmee: Houston Astros, (407) 933-2520
Plant City: Cincinnati Reds, (513) 421-4510
Port St. Lucie: New York Mets, (407) 879-7378
St. Petersburg: St. Louis Cardinals, (813) 822-3384
Vero Beach: Los Angeles Dodgers, (407) 569-4900
West Palm Beach: Atlanta Braves, (407) 683-6100, and Montreal
    Expos, (407) 689-9122

ITINERARY

DAY 1   Founded in 1565, St. Augustine is the oldest colonial settlement in what is now the United States. As you explore its massive stone fortress and restored historic district, let your imagination run free and recall the colorful era of pirates and treasure-laden Spanish galleons.

DAY 2   Today is beach day. En route from St. Augustine to the Space Coast, you'll find a surprising variety of beaches—Flagler Beach, Ormond Beach, Daytona Beach, New Smyrna Beach, and Canaveral National Seashore's Apollo and Klondike beaches, to name just a few. Whether you prefer a crowded, lively beach scene or total seclusion, you'll find a perfect sun-bathing spot today.

DAY 3   Visit Spaceport USA at Kennedy Space Center, where you'll see a large collection of astronaut and space probe memorabilia on display. You can also watch a film of a space shuttle launch on a giant IMAX screen and take a two-hour tour of the space center. Later, drive out to Merritt Island National Wildlife Refuge to see myriad birds and maybe alligators. Leave by mid-afternoon and drive to Walt Disney World.

DAYS 4 and 5   Walt Disney World is the largest commercial tourist attraction on earth, a seemingly endless array of all the family-style thrills that a multibillion-dollar budget can buy. It would take a full week to see everything here. If you're traveling with preteen children (and plenty of money), plan to spend extra time at Walt Disney World, omitting other destinations in this itinerary if necessary. For travelers with time or budget limitations, our strategy lets you experience a generous sample of "the World" in just two days. You'll see the futuristic and the foreign at Epcot Center on Day 4. Day 5 presents a tough choice: whether to take a nostalgic trip through the Magic Kingdom or tour the newly opened MGM-Disney Studios.

DAY 6   You can drive from Walt Disney World to Palm Beach in about three hours on Florida's Turnpike, but why spend your vacation on freeways? Here is an all-day "blue highways" scenic route that will take you through orange groves, the lake district, and the Seminole Indian reservation.

DAY 7   Florida's Gold Coast—the solid wall of resort hotels and condominiums from Palm Beach to Miami Beach—is the focus of today's explorations. This morning you'll get a voyeuristic look at the life-styles of the rich and famous at Palm Beach—mansions and one of the most expensive shopping districts on earth. By evening, you'll be set up in one of Miami Beach's restored Art Deco hotels, perhaps not the most expensive accommodations on the Gold Coast but certainly the most unusual.

DAY 8 As you wander around Miami Beach, you'll see pastel examples of "Tropical Deco" architecture everywhere, so unique that the Deco District has been designated a National Historic Area even though most structures are less than 50 years old. As intriguing as the buildings are the residents of Miami Beach, a people-watcher's feast of artists, yuppies, media figures, aging hippies, senior citizens, Caribbean refugees, and one-of-a-kind eccentrics. Stroll the beach, the parks where wild parrots live, the art galleries and boutiques. Bask in the energy of this offbeat community.

DAY 9 Miami is not Miami Beach. Miami is a huge, sparkling white, modern city with such a large Spanish-speaking population that it is often called "the capital of Latin America." Everything you've heard about Miami is most likely true, but this city defies stereotypes. Today's auto tour includes such diverse destinations as Vizcaya (a lavish palace museum), Coral Gables' Venetian Pool (a former stone quarry that has been converted to the most ornate swimming pool anywhere), and Little Havana (which, contrary to many visitors' expectations, is not a slum).

DAY 10 Drive the Overseas Highway all the way to Key West. Along the way, you'll have an opportunity to explore the only living coral reef in U.S. waters at John Pennekamp Coral Reef State Park, a perfect place to try snorkeling or take a glass-bottom boat tour. You'll reach Key West, the southernmost point in the continental United States, in time for the daily sunset celebration at Mallory Square Dock.

DAY 11 Explore Key West. See where Ernest Hemingway lived, where Tennessee Williams lived, and where John James Audubon didn't live. Visit two museums that display the fruits of early-day "wrecking" and modern treasure hunting; fondle a bar of gold. Stand on the southernmost point in the continental United States. Finish the day with a sentimental pilgrimage to Hemingway's favorite bar. Then (in a properly literary spirit) stumble across the street to Hemingway's other favorite bar.

DAY 12 Return to the mainland by the same highway that brought you—it's the only one. Along the way, sightseeing possibilities include a wildlife refuge that is home to the tiny Key deer, a botanical preserve accessible only by passenger ferry, and a dolphin research center.

DAY 13   Everglades National Park preserves an ecosystem that is unique in the world, a 50-mile-wide river of grass studded with small islands—hardwood "hammocks" and pine-forested "keys"—and fringed by a mangrove maze. Wildlife abounds. The single park road from the entrance gate to Flamingo lets you see a cross section of the national park on a series of board-walks. To experience more, rent a canoe or take a tour boat cruise on Florida Bay.

DAY 14   As you drive the Tamiami Trail, formerly the main route between Miami and the Gulf Coast, visit the Miccosukee Indians' cultural center and take time to explore Big Cypress National Preserve, created to protect the watershed for Ever-glades National Park and the last habitat of the Florida panther. See dark, strange cypress swamps dripping with Spanish moss and bedecked with orchids. If you'd like to take an airboat ride through the everglades, here's your chance.

DAY 15   In the morning, visit Corkscrew Swamp, a National Audubon Society preserve. From a two-mile boardwalk safely above water (and 'gator) level, you'll have your best chance to view the abundant wildlife of the cypress swamps. In the after-noon, see Thomas Edison's winter home, laboratory, and gardens. Then drive out to Sanibel and Captiva islands, which boast the best shell-hunting beaches in the United States.

DAY 16   Sarasota's feature attraction is the three-ring Ringling Museums. Great art, ostentatious architecture, and the circus make for a full day.

DAY 17   Start with a walking tour of St. Petersburg, where a top highlight is the Salvador Dali Museum. Later in the day, hit the beach or drive down to Bradenton to visit a manatee and see a laser lightshow.

DAY 18   Drive to Ocala, about a hundred miles to the north in the center of the state. The coastal segment of the route takes you through the Greek sponge-divers' village of Tarpon Springs, past two venerable Gulf Coast attractions, Homosassa Springs (a natural "fishbowl") and Weeki Wachee (your only chance on this trip to see mermaids), to Crystal River Archaeo-logical Site, where mounds much like Mayan pyramids bear wit-ness to a lost civilization.

DAY 19 Many visitors to the Ocala area spend their whole day pleasurably at Silver Springs, the oldest tourist attraction in Florida. But there are many other possibilities around Ocala besides glass-bottom boats. Ocala National Forest offers some of the best hiking and canoeing in the state as well as hidden lakes and artesian springs in which to swim. On the return trip, make a short detour through Cross Creek, the home of Florida's most beloved author. (No, not Ernest Hemingway.)

DAY 20 Return to the Gulf Coast to visit Cedar Key, formerly one of the largest port cities in Florida, now a quiet little cabin community and wildlife refuge. Back on the mainland, see Manatee Springs State Park, an idyllic spot for swimming or canoeing, 'way down upon the Suwannee River.

DAY 21 As you drive north from the Suwannee River to the Tallahassee area, back roads beckon toward Florida's "hidden coast," most of which is only accessible by boat. Your destination is beautiful Wakulla Springs, once a private estate, now a public park. Spend the night at Wakulla Springs Lodge or camp at Alligator Point, where you can have miles of sugar-white beach to yourself.

DAY 22 In Tallahassee, the state capital, pause to think back over your trip. Consider, as legislators must when they meet in this soft-spoken, very Southern city so unlike any other place in Florida, the state's explosive growth, environmental dilemmas, and cultural collisions. Then drive on.

ST. AUGUSTINE

The Florida peninsula dangles from Interstate 10 like a Christmas stocking. This itinerary starts at the eastern end of I-10 and will return to Tallahassee, four hours west on I-10, three weeks and 1,800 miles from now. If you are arriving in Florida from the north via Interstate 95 or from the west via Interstates 75 and 10, read on. If you're starting from someplace else in Florida—for example, the Orlando area (Day 4), the Miami area (Day 8), or the Tampa Bay area (Day 17)—turn to that section, and after Day 22 return here via I-10.

The oldest continuously occupied town in the United States, founded in 1565, St. Augustine was for centuries the northernmost Spanish seaport in America, a stronghold against the pirates who robbed ships of the gold that conquistadores had plundered from Mexico and Peru. The town has a massive castlelike fortress, practically every building over 150 years old in the state, a population of 15,000, and a wealth of gory history and farfetched legends to breathe life into the ancient walls.

Suggested Schedule	
Morning	Drive to St. Augustine.
11:00 a.m.	Arrive in St. Augustine. Visit Castillo de San Marcos.
1:00 p.m.	Lunch.
2:00 p.m.	Explore St. Augustine's historic district.
Evening	Dinner and a moonlight stroll.
	Spend the night in St. Augustine or camp nearby.

Amelia Island

If you are arriving in Florida from the north via Interstate 95, avoid Jacksonville's freeway maze by exiting 13 miles south of the state line, taking Highway 200 east to Fernandina Beach (13 miles) and then following Highway A1A south along the coastal barrier islands for 55 miles to St. Augustine.

The town of Fernandina (pop. 8,000), which occupies the north half of Amelia Island, was one of the largest port cities in Florida a century ago, back when Miami and the Gold Coast were impenetrable, uninhabitable mangrove jungle. Florida's first railroad linked Fernandina to another major port of that era, Cedar Key (Day 20), across the peninsula on the Gulf Coast.

For 300 years, French, Spanish, Mexican, English, Yankees, Confederates, and local free-lance "patriots" fought over, occupied, frequently renamed, and occasionally burned Amelia Island. Its port, Fernandina, was a hideout for smugglers and pirates including Jean Lafitte, Captain Kidd, and Blackbeard. U.S. President James Monroe, while promoting a covert operation to overthrow the Spanish government there, called Fernandina a "festering fleshpot."

Modern-day tourism and commerce have practically bypassed the town, and today the main industry is shrimp fishing. A major restoration effort is under way in Fernandina's 30-block historic district. Stop at the Chamber of Commerce in the old railroad depot at First and Centre streets to pick up a free "Centre St. Fernandina Historic District" booklet. Follow the booklet's suggested walking or driving tour, or, for a quicker visit, proceed up Centre Street to Seventh and turn right to see four blocks of elegant old mansions.

As you follow Highway A1A south from Fernandina, you'll pass Amelia Island Plantation, Florida's northernmost major resort complex and one of the finest in the state. Amid dense live oak forests, sand dunes, lagoons, and tidal marshlands, the 1,250-acre resort offers golf, tennis, horseback riding, biking, fishing, and an uncrowded, seemingly endless beach, as well as rooms, which start at about $120 per night for a double (about 20 percent higher during the peak season, mid-March through May). Special discount packages are available for four- or five-night stays and for families. If you'd like reservation information, call (800) 342-6841 from Florida, (800) 874-6878 nationwide. Even if you can't stay, take a few extra minutes to drive through, admire how the graceful landscaping makes the most of natural beauty, and say a silent "thanks" to Charles Fraser, who developed the resort in the 1960s. He bought the property from Union Carbide, which had planned to strip-mine it for potassium.

A ferry takes you across the St. Johns River from Fort George Island to Mayport; it runs every half-hour from 6:20 a.m. to 10:00 p.m. and costs $1.50 per vehicle.

Travel Route: Jacksonville Area to St. Augustine (41 miles)

If you are coming from the west on Interstate 10, stay on it. The right lanes of I-10 become Interstate 95 South in the center of downtown Jacksonville, just before the long bridge across the St. Johns River. After crossing the river, stay on I-95 South for 16 miles to the US 1 South exit for St. Augustine. From there, it's an uneventful, billboard-decorated 25-mile drive.

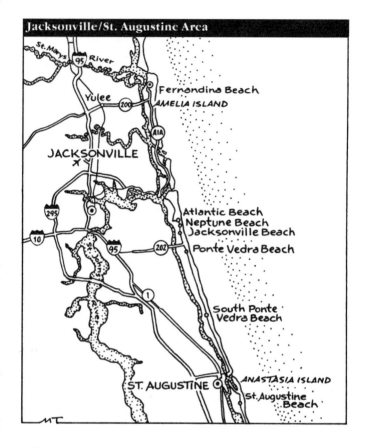

Jacksonville/St. Augustine Area

If you have extra time and can't wait to see the ocean, exit
I-95 on J. T. Butler Boulevard (Highway 202) and drive east to
join coastal Highway A1A, which takes you to St. Augustine, at
Ponte Vedra Beach.

If you find yourself disoriented in Jacksonville, remember
that all limited-access freeways eventually lead to I-95. Once
you've crossed the St. Johns River on any downtown bridge,
any major eastbound street eventually leads to the Atlantic
Ocean and Highway A1A.

Getting Around St. Augustine

Explore old St. Augustine on foot. Park at Castillo de San
Marcos. (Other parking lots are nearby at the Chamber of Commerce and just inside the Old City Gate.) After touring the fortress, walk a block west and cross the highway to the Old City

Gate. Walking is the best way to see St. Augustine's historic district; St. George, the district's main street, is closed to private vehicles.

Sightseeing tours also cover the major sights as well as some minor ones you might choose to skip if you explore independently. There are tan-and-red open-air "trains" (St. Augustine Sightseeing Trains, 829-6545), green-and-white "trolleys" (St. Augustine Historical Tours, 829-3800), and horse-drawn carriages (Colee's Sightseeing Carriage Tours, 829-2818). Tour prices range up to about $25 per adult for all-day tours, but all three tour companies offer basic one-hour tours of the Old City for $7 per adult and $2 per child age 6 to 12. Both the train and the trolley let you get off and visit attractions at your leisure, then board a later tour on the same ticket. They run every 15 to 20 minutes until 6:00 p.m.

St. Augustine Sightseeing Highlights

▲▲▲ **Castillo de San Marcos National Monument**—This fortress, built between 1672 and 1695 from blocks of resilient coquina limestone, has withstood flaming arrows, cannonballs, hurricanes, and, in the twentieth century, the footsteps of up to a million tourists each year. It is the only structure in St. Augustine (or Florida) that was built before 1700. Explore the dank rooms and passageways between the exterior and interior walls. Marvel at how 1,500 people could have lived in the central courtyard for 50 days during a seige. Stand on the ramparts, take aim at the distant Atlantic down a cannon barrel, and imagine pirate ships. The castillo is open daily from 8:30 a.m. to 5:15 p.m. November through March, 9:00 a.m. to 5:45 p.m. the rest of the year. Admission is $1 for adults, free for children under 16 when accompanied by an adult.

▲▲▲ **Spanish Quarter**—The heart of the historic district is the state-operated living museum created by historian Earle W. Newton, who is also known for his restoration of Old Sturbridge Village in Massachusetts. It is located along St. George Street between Fort Alley and Cuna Street. Guides in period dress will show you through a half-dozen antique-furnished eighteenth-century homes and tell you about everyday life in Spanish colonial times. Enter through the Triay House at 29 St. George Street. Admission is $2.50 for adults, $1.50 for children and students (ages 6 to 18), or $5 per family. Hours are 9:00 a.m. to 5:00 p.m. daily.

▲▲ **Historic District Walking Tour**—When you leave the living museum, continue south on St. George for two blocks to the **Sanchez House**, built by an early cattle baron. Admission is free. Hours are 9:30 a.m. to 5:00 p.m., closed Thursdays. Continue south for one more block and turn left on Cathedral Street

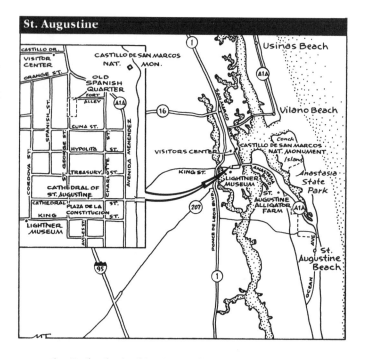

to see the **Cathedral of St. Augustine**. The original church on
this site, one of the oldest Catholic churches in the United
States, built in 1790, was partly destroyed by fire in 1887, but its
ruins form the nave of the present cathedral. In front of the
cathedral is the **Plaza de la Constitución**, the old town
square. An open-air marketplace is re-created at the east end of
the plaza, where in past centuries slaves, too, were bought and
sold.

Walk up King Street, which bounds the plaza on the south, to
Cordova Street (one block west of St. George) to see a pair of
posh former resort hotels built by railroad tycoon Henry
Flagler, the father of Florida tourism, whose name and accom-
plishments you'll encounter all the way from here to Key West.
The **Lightner Museum** and adjoining City Hall, at King and
Cordova streets, were originally the Hotel Alcazar, which Flagler
built in 1888-89. The hotel closed during World War II, and
Chicago publisher Otto C. Lightner bought it to house his
collections—antique music boxes, stained glass, and crystal as
well as Art Nouveau and oriental works. There are also a Victorian Village and natural history exhibits. The old hotel's
indoor swimming pool area and casino have been converted

into a mall where antiques are for sale. Admission to the museum is $3 for adults and $.75 for students ages 12 to 18. Hours are 9:00 a.m. to 5:00 p.m. daily. Across King Street from the museum is **Flagler College**, formerly the elegant Ponce de Leon Hotel. The front courtyard is open to the public.

A block down King Street from the Lightner Museum/City Hall complex is **Zordaya Castle**, a modern reproduction of the Alhambra, the great Moorish castle in Granada, Spain. Here, if you wish, you can take a tour and see what twelfth-century harem quarters looked like. Also on display are antique mosaics and such bizarre Egyptian collectibles as a mummy's foot and a 2,300-year-old rug woven from the hair of giant cats.

To return to the historic district, walk two blocks north on Cordova Street and turn right (east) on Treasury Street, one of the town's narrow, picturesque side streets, which will return you to St. George Street near the Sanchez House, four blocks south of the old city gates.

▲**St. Augustine Alligator Farm**—"Old" is a magic word in St. Augustine. Around town, you'll find the Old Jail, the Old Spanish Cemetery, the Oldest Wooden Schoolhouse, the Oldest Store, the Oldest House. An often overlooked oldie is "the World's Original Alligator Attraction" (established in 1893), the granddaddy of all the wild animal theme parks in Florida. Farms like this one offered visitors their only chance to see alligators when they were on the brink of extinction in the wild. By satisfying the demand for alligator handbags, wallets, and cowboy boots, such farms helped save the skins of wild alligators, which have now multiplied their way off the endangered species list. You're almost sure to see a wild alligator at Everglades National Park (Day 13) or Corkscrew Swamp (Day 15); but if you'd like to see *lots* of alligators, as well as crocodiles, ostriches, monkeys, deer, ducks, goats, and native birds, here they are. The alligator farm is located on Anastasia Island at Highway A1A (Anastasia Boulevard) and Young Avenue. Admission is $5.50 per adult, $5 for seniors over 55, and $3.50 for children ages 3 to 11. Hours are 9:00 a.m. to 5:30 p.m. daily.

Food
Lunch is easy in St. Augustine. As you walk down St. George Street, simply look at the menus and blackboards posted outside the many small restaurants until you see something irresistible. Since this town sees many more day-trippers than overnighters, most Old Town restaurants close by 5:00 p.m.

For dinner, one of the best seafood restaurants in town is **Saltwater Cowboys**, on Dondanville Road in St. Augustine Beach, open daily from 5:00 to 10:00 p.m., 471-2332. Generous seafood dinners run $10 to $15. Unpretentious, extremely

affordable, and usually crowded during the dinner hour,
O'Steens serves up the best shrimp dinners in St. Augustine.
It's at 205 Anastasia Boulevard, 829-6974, open Monday
through Saturday from 11:00 a.m. to 8:30 p.m., no reservations.
El Toro con Sombrero, 10 Anastasia Boulevard (near the east
end of the Bridge of Lions), 842-8852, serves inexpensive Mexican food. Its location fits in perfectly with a romantic moonlight stroll, and it's open late—until 1:00 a.m. daily.

Lodging

While visiting historic St. Augustine, why not stay in a historic
bed and breakfast? The old town has several, and you'll want to
make reservations at one of them weeks in advance. Top of the
line is **Casa de Solana**, 21 Aviles Street, (904) 824-3555. Near
the Oldest Store Museum, this restored, antique-filled 1763
Spanish colonial house has just four luxurious guest suites at
about $100 a night. In the same price range and a short distance
farther south is the **Westcott House**, 146 Avenida Merendez,
(904) 824-4301. B&B accommodations in the $45 to $70 range
can be arranged at the **Kenwood Inn**, 1½ blocks south of the
Bridge of Lions at 38 Marine Street, (904) 824-2116. Also worth
contacting is the **St. Francis Inn**, 279 St. George Street at the
corner of St. Francis Street, (904) 824-6068. This 1791 home
rents rooms for about $50 a night. The best B&B bargain in
town, if you can book one of the two rooms there, is **Sailor's
Rest**, 298 St. George Street, (904) 824-3817, rates from $35.
None of these places accepts pets, and some may not want small
children.

No reservations? Brand-name motels line US 1 north of town,
and more can be found along Ocean Avenue on St. Augustine
Beach. Rates are typically $50 to $70 a night—slightly higher on
the beach than beside the highway. "No vacancy" signs are
rarely a problem.

Camping

The most convenient public campground is **Anastasia State
Recreation Area** in the town of St. Augustine Beach, 4 miles
from the Bridge of Lions on Highway A1A. Turn left just past the
alligator farm. The park has a beach, sand dunes, and 140 campsites that cost about $15 per night with electric hookups. No
pets are allowed.

The **KOA St. Augustine Beach** is at 525 Pope Road (follow
the signs from Highway A1A), about eight blocks from the
beach. Campsites with all the amenities, including satellite TV
hookups, start at $16 a night.

ATLANTIC COAST BEACHES

An assortment of beaches, from hectic Daytona to sublime Klondike, line Highway A1A. Choose the one that sounds best to you. If you're traveling with children, spend the morning at Marineland. Otherwise, you may want to visit the sights of Ormond Beach, including John D. Rockefeller's house. In either case, set aside enough time to get wet, get started on your suntan, and get sand between your toes.

Suggested Schedule

9:00 a.m.	Drive from St. Augustine to Marineland or the beach of your choice.
9:30 a.m.	Visit Marineland or lie on the beach.
12:00 noon	Lunch.
1:00 p.m.	Drive on. Visit the Rockefeller mansion in Ormond Beach or stop at Daytona Beach, New Smyrna Beach, or Canaveral National Seashore.
4:00 p.m.	Check into your accommodations or set up camp.
4:30 p.m.	Back to the beach? Spend the night at Ormond Beach, Daytona Beach, or New Smyrna Beach.

Travel Route: St. Augustine to Canaveral National Seashore (85 miles)
From St. Augustine Beach, follow Highway A1A down the coast for 62 miles to South Daytona Beach, where you'll cross a bridge back to the mainland and join US 1. Nine miles south on US 1 is New Smyrna Beach and the turnoff to the north entrance of Canaveral National Seashore.

Sightseeing Highlights
▲▲**Anastasia Island**—To reach St. Augustine Beach, follow Highway A1A (Cathedral Street on the mainland side, Anastasia Boulevard on the island side) across the Bridge of Lions.
Anastasia State Recreation Area, the best public swimming beach in town, is 4 miles down the highway.

If St. Augustine's Spanish colonial history intrigues you, stop ten miles farther along Highway A1A at **Fort Matanzas National Monument**, a fortress tower that was built as an outpost of Castillo de San Marcos. The name Matanzas comes from a Spanish word meaning ''slaughter''; on this site, St. Augustine's

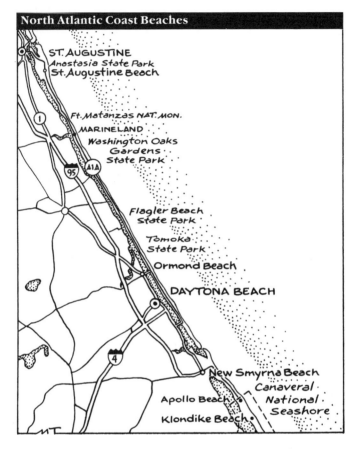

North Atlantic Coast Beaches

ST. AUGUSTINE
Anastasia State Park
St. Augustine Beach

Ft. Matanzas NAT. MON.
MARINELAND
Washington Oaks
Gardens
State Park

Flagler Beach
State Park

Tomoka
State Park

Ormond Beach

DAYTONA BEACH

New Smyrna Beach
Canaveral
National
Seashore

Apollo Beach

Klondike Beach

founding conquistadores wiped out shipwrecked French
Huguenots in 1565. Fort Matanzas is not a good swimming spot.
It is situated on a narrow inlet with potentially deadly currents.

▲▲ **Marineland**—Four miles south of Fort Matanzas on Highway A1A, 18 miles south of St. Augustine, is Marineland of
Florida, the original marine life theme park, established in 1938,
now on the National Register of Historic Places. Trained dolphins still perform and seem to enjoy it as much as the specta-
tors do. Other acts feature sea lions, otters, and penguins, and
this is one of the few places in Florida where you can get a
close-up view of a flamingo. Exhibits re-create a tropical reef
and a freshwater spring. A 3-D film, *Sea Dreams*, takes viewers
on a plunge from the clouds down into the ocean depths.
Admission, which covers all attractions in the park, is $7.95 per

adult, $3.95 for children ages 3 to 11. Hours are 9:00 a.m. to 5:00 p.m. daily.

▲**Washington Oaks Gardens State Park**—This small state park is on the west side of A1A about 2 miles south of Marineland. Besides landscaped flower gardens, the park preserves a fragment of the natural vegetation that covered this part of the coast in earlier centuries—a wind-twisted scrub oak forest and a hardwood hammock dripping with Spanish moss. Stroll the peaceful, easy nature trail.

▲**Flagler Beach State Park**—Seventeen miles south of Marineland, this is the showpiece beach of the Florida state park system, as nearly pristine as you're likely to find along Highway A1A. The beach memorializes Henry Flagler, one of the most influential figures in Florida history. A retired executive of John D. Rockefeller's Standard Oil Company, he built the railroad that ran from Jacksonville all the way down the Atlantic Coast, following approximately the same route as today's Highway A1A. As he completed each segment of the railroad, he established one resort hotel after another so that passengers would have someplace to go on his trains. Besides his lavish hotels in St. Augustine and the Ormond Hotel in Ormond Beach (see below), Flagler founded both Palm Beach (where he built his own mansion) and Miami (where the downtown main street is named after him). Not content with having converted south Florida's mangrove jungle coastline into prime beachfront property (much of which he owned), Flagler constructed the Overseas Railroad from island to island, all the way to Key West, laying the roadbed for what is now the Overseas Highway (US 1). He planned to continue the railroad to Cuba but didn't live long enough.

▲▲**Ormond Beach**—The major sightseeing attractions of this beach town are not on the beach; they are along East Granada Avenue, which runs between the beach and the bridge to the mainland. To find them, as you're traveling south along Highway A1A (Ocean Shore Boulevard), turn right (west) at Granada Plaza just past the Oceanside Country Club golf course.

Now a suburb of Daytona Beach, Ormond Beach is where auto racing began. As early as 1902, pioneer race drivers like Alex Winston and Barney Oldfield were speed-testing their machines on a measured mile course along Ormond Beach's hard-packed sand, setting a series of world speed records there: 57 mph in 1902, 120 mph in 1906, nearly 277 mph by 1935. You can see photos and memorabilia of early-day racing as well as a few antique race cars (including an operational replica of the Stanley Steamer Rocket, which reached a speed of 197 mph in 1907—just before it crashed) at the **Birthplace of Speed Museum**, housed in an old fire station at 160 East Granada.

Admission is $1 per person. Hours are Tuesday through Saturday, 10:00 a.m. to 5:00 p.m.

A block west of the speed museum, across the street from a plaque marking the site where the original "birthplace of speed" garage burned down, is the **Ormond Memorial Art Museum and Gardens**, 78 East Granada. The four-and-a-half-acre botanical garden, laid out after World War II by the same man who created London's Kew Gardens, is said to be the most popular place in the United States for outdoor weddings. The art museum houses over 60 paintings on spiritual themes by artist Malcom Fraser, as well as changing exhibits of local art. The strange-looking little museum building, which blends oriental architecture with latticework, is open 12:00 noon to 5:00 p.m. daily except Wednesdays, closed Thanksgiving, Christmas Day, New Year's Day, Easter, and the month of August. Admission to both the gardens and the museum is free.

The premier Ormond Beach attraction is **The Casements** at East Granada and Riverside Drive, a few blocks west of the speed museum on the same side of the street. This mansion was John D. Rockefeller's winter home from 1914 to 1937, when he died here. It now serves as a cultural center, featuring an odd assortment of exhibits such as Boy Scout memorabilia and Hungarian folk art. Admission and tours are free; donations are welcome. The Casements is open to the public Monday through Saturday from 9:00 a.m. to 12:00 noon, closed on holidays. Guided tours are also conducted on weekday afternoons; call 673-4701 for the current tour schedule.

Across the street from the Casements, the old **Ormond Hotel** dates back to 1888. Henry Flagler bought the hotel four years later and expanded it. In its day, it was the largest wooden building in the world. Besides neighbor Rockefeller, who used to play golf here, guests included Mrs. Ulysses S. Grant, Cornelius Vanderbilt, Henry Ford, John Jacob Astor, President Warren G. Harding, and Will Rogers. The hotel deteriorated and finally was sold in foreclosure in 1987. By the time you read this, it could be (a) another museum, (b) an elegantly restored resort hotel, (c) still boarded up, or (d) gone. An outspoken Save the Hotel group has been fighting for years to prevent the last possibility.

▲▲**Daytona Beach**—This town's name is synonymous with fast cars. It started with the local pastime of drag racing on the beach. In 1959, the racing events were moved to the new Daytona International Speedway, now the most famous auto racecourse besides Indianapolis. The beach, the town, and all 436 hotels and motels, are standing-room-only during Speed Weeks, the series of racing events that begin around February 1 and climax during the third week of February with the Daytona

500. Unless you have arranged lodging reservations far in advance, it's best to detour around the Daytona area on Interstate 95 during this peak of the winter auto racing season. If you'd like to attend one of the Speed Weeks races, contact the speedway at (904) 253-6711 for ticket information. You can drive your car on the same hard-packed beach where they used to race. The speed limit is now 10 mph. While admission to the beach is free, there is a $3 charge to park there.

Finding accommodations is also a problem in mid-March, when college students from all over the eastern United States gather for the traditional rites of spring. Daytona Beach is the destination of choice for the raucous week-long spring break burst of young bodies awash in suntan lotion, beer, and other substances. No motel room? Don't worry—just stay up all night like everyone else. (If it *does* worry you, take the freeway and stop elsewhere.)

▲**New Smyrna Beach**—Overshadowed by the booming resort areas of Daytona Beach to the north and the Space Coast to the south, New Smyrna Beach seems perpetually in search of an identity. It has been characterized by various promoters as "The World's Widest Beach" (it is said to be a mile wide at extreme low tide) and "The World's Safest Beach"; it may also be the hardest to find, since the town of New Smyrna Beach is ten minutes west of the beach itself. Keep your eyes peeled for the sign marking the turnoff on your right. You can drive your car on New Smyrna Beach, too, but there the similarity to Daytona Beach ends. The seashore at New Smyrna is not crowded. Birds normally outnumber humans here, and the people you'll encounter along the sand—local families and retirees—may blink in amazement at the presence of a genuine tourist (it is a source of pride among residents that New Smyrna Beach is "not too close" to central Florida's major tourist attractions).

▲▲**Canaveral National Seashore: Apollo and Klondike Beaches**—If it's total seclusion you're after, continue south beyond New Smyrna Beach (the beach, not the town) on the same road, also designated Highway A1A although it's a dead-end, to reach the north entrance of Canaveral National Seashore. After taking you past the information center and two Indian shell mounds accessible by short interpretive trails, the road along Apollo Beach ends, and the beach changes its name. No vehicles are allowed on 12-mile Klondike Beach, and if you walk far enough south along the shore, yours will be the only footprints in the sand. There is no fresh water on Klondike Beach, so bring your own, as well as sunscreen and insect repellent. Admission to Canaveral National Seashore is $3 per vehicle. The seashore access road opens at 6:30 a.m. and closes at dusk; the information center is open daily from 8:00 a.m. to 4:30 p.m.

Food

You can find all kinds of cuisine in Daytona Beach. A local favorite for over 40 years, **Gene's Steak House** on US 92, 255-2059, serves tender cuts of high-quality beef and sometimes offers seafood specials. For Chinese and Japanese food, it's the **Asian Inn** at 2516 South Atlantic Avenue (Highway A1A) in the Atlantic Plaza Shopping Center, 788-6269, open daily from 3:00 p.m. to 2:00 a.m. Northern Italian food is served at **Ricardo's**, 610 Glenview Boulevard, 253-3035, open daily from 5:00 p.m. to 10:30 p.m. For a restaurant with a genuinely unusual flavor, try the **Hungarian Village**, 424 South Ridgewood Avenue (US 1), 253-5712, open daily from 5:00 p.m. to 10:00 p.m. As far as we can ascertain, this is the only Hungarian restaurant in Florida; even Walt Disney World doesn't have one.

For good food on a tight budget, in Daytona Beach go to **Morrison's Cafeteria** at 200 North Ridgewood Avenue, 258-6396, or the **Piccadilly Cafeteria** in the Volusia Mall on US 92, 258-5373. Both are open daily from 11:00 a.m. to 8:30 p.m.

Lodging

Resort hotels line Daytona Beach. Top of the line, and one of the few hotels on the beach with architecture that isn't entirely rectangular, is the **Daytona Hilton**, 2637 South Atlantic Avenue, (904) 767-7350. Rooms start around $100 a night. If all you need is a bed and a bit of beachfront, several apartment motels along Atlantic Avenue (Highway A1A) offer accommodations starting at less than $50 a night in season. Try the **Famous Inn Motel**, 3703 South Atlantic Avenue, (904) 767-3182, the **Castaway Beach Resort**, 2075 South Atlantic Avenue, (904) 255-6461, or the **Beacon By The Sea Motel**, 1803 South Atlantic Avenue, (904) 255-3619. Nearby in Ormond Beach, motels in the same price range include the **Driftwood Beach Motel**, 657 South Atlantic Avenue, (904) 677-1331, and the **Casa Del Mar**, 621 South Atlantic Avenue, (904) 672-4550.

In New Smyrna Beach, a beautifully restored historic hotel fronting on the Intercoastal Waterway is the **Riverview Hotel**, just over the North Causeway Bridge at 103 Flagler Avenue, (904) 428-5858. For the budget-minded, New Smyrna also has several modest motels along US 1 on the north side of town with rooms in the $30 to $40 range.

Camping

Look for public camping in the Ormond/Daytona/New Smyrna area at **Tomoka State Park**, 3 miles north of Ormond Beach via North Beach Street. There are nature trails, and boats, canoes, and bicycles are for rent. Sites cost about $15 per night.

The **KOA Daytona South/New Smyrna Beach** is located at 1300 Old Mission Road, which is off Highway 44 a little more than a mile west of US 1. Call (904) 427-3581. This campground is several miles from the beach but also a comfortable distance from major highways. Sites start around $18 per night.

KENNEDY SPACE CENTER AND
CANAVERAL NATIONAL SEASHORE

The first explorer to set foot in Florida, in 1513, was Juan Ponce de Leon, a retired governor of Puerto Rico who had sailed with Columbus. Modern historians believe he landed on Cape Canaveral, not St. Augustine as previously thought, and that he was searching not for a "fountain of youth" but for an island of which he'd been appointed governor sight unseen. Ponce de Leon never found his island or his lost youth.

Today, Cape Canaveral is the place where explorations of the solar system begin. Yet the seashore and wildlife refuge just over the space center fence have changed little since Ponce de Leon's time.

Suggested Schedule

9:00 a.m.	Drive to Kennedy Space Center.
10:00 a.m.	Visit Spaceport USA.
11:00 a.m.	Ride the Earth Shuttle.
1:00 p.m.	Take a scenic drive on Merritt Island and picnic on Playalinda Beach.
2:00 p.m.	Drive to Walt Disney World.
3:00 p.m.	Check into your Walt Disney World hotel or campground for a three-night stay.

Travel Route: New Smyrna Beach to Kennedy Space Center (46 miles) to Walt Disney World (54 miles)

From New Smyrna Beach, take Highway 44 west to Interstate 95 and go 34 miles south on I-95 to the clearly marked Highway 405 exit for Kennedy Space Center. Highway 405 crosses the Inland Waterway and takes you directly to Spaceport USA.

When you leave Kennedy Space Center, if you wish to visit Merritt Island and Playalinda Beach, as soon as you cross the Indian River back to the mainland turn right (north) on US 1. Follow it along the shoreline through Titusville and watch for the left turn to Canaveral National Seashore (Highway 406).

Returning from Merritt Island and Canaveral National Seashore, follow Highway 406 straight through Titusville to I-95 South and take the interstate south to the second interchange, Highway 407. (If you're driving directly from Spaceport USA to Disney World, you don't need to get back on the interstate. You can catch Highway 407 by taking a left turn 3 miles after you return to the mainland; in 2 more miles you'll cross the interstate.)

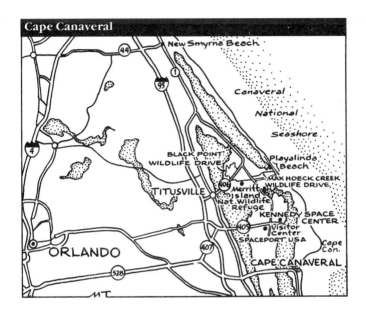

Highway 407 takes you 4 miles from I-95 to the entrance to the Bee Line Expressway (Highway 528), a fast turnpike that takes you straight to Interstate 4, just two exits north of Walt Disney World, in about half an hour.

Sightseeing Highlights
▲▲▲**John F. Kennedy Space Center**—Spaceport USA, the Kennedy Space Center information station, may be the most elaborate federal visitor center anywhere. Here you'll find extensive exhibits of the Right Stuff, including spacecraft, space suits, and moon rocks as well as a Florida wildlife exhibit, an art gallery displaying paintings, photographs, and sculptures commissioned by the NASA Art Program, and a new Satellites and You exhibit that uses animatronics and multimedia effects to simulate working conditions on a space station of the near future. If you're not fortunate enough to witness an actual space shuttle launch, the next best thing is Spaceport USA's 37-minute IMAX film, *The Dream Is Alive*, which shows a shuttle launch and footage shot from space on a screen nearly six stories tall. Admission to the IMAX theater is $2.75 per adult and $1.75 for children ages 3 to 12. The other Spaceport USA exhibits are free. Hours are 8:00 a.m. to dusk daily except Christmas Day. (The center also closes part or all day on space shuttle launch or landing days. You can get up-to-date launch information toll-free, only from within Florida, by calling 800-432-2153.)

Earth Shuttle bus tours run from Spaceport USA, taking visitors around the space center. The two-hour tours include Complex 39, the space shuttle launch pad, and the 525-foot-high vehicle assembly building. The tour route varies, since some areas are off-limits during launch preparations, but may include the flight crew training building, the Air Force Space Museum, and/or several historic and present-day launch pads for missiles, satellites, and spacecraft. The tour costs $4 per adult and $1.75 for children ages 3 to 12. Tour buses leave frequently beginning at 9:00 a.m., with the last departure approximately two hours before sunset.

▲▲ **Merritt Island National Wildlife Refuge and Playalinda Beach**—Immune from development because of the intermittent hazard posed by large rockets roaring overhead, Merritt Island is one of Florida's most important wildlife refuges because of the large number of migrating birds that spend the winter here. For example, the island supports from 50,000 to 70,000 ducks and over 100,000 coots. The 280 species of birds that spend at least part of the year here also include seagulls, sandpipers, egrets, ibises, osprey, the endangered southern bald eagle, and the formerly endangered brown pelican, which has made such a successful comeback that it is now commonly seen everywhere along the Florida coast. Four kinds of sea turtles, two kinds of harmless snakes, and the West Indian manatee round out the list of endangered species that make their homes on and around Merritt Island. Other denizens of the island are alligators, raccoons, bobcats, armadillos, and assorted snakes.

Armed with a good pair of binoculars, you can see many species of waterfowl along the unpaved **Black Point Wildlife Drive**, a left turn from Highway 406 about a mile past where Highway 402 forks off to the right toward the beach. Allow 30 minutes for the wildlife drive, and add on another hour if you wish to hike the 2-mile Cruickshank Trail, a loop from the trailhead midway along the wildlife drive. When the drive returns to Highway 406, turn right and return to the fork in the road; make a hard left onto Highway 402, which takes you past the space shuttle landing area (on your right), through the Canaveral National Seashore entrance gate (open 6:30 a.m. to dusk, admission $3 per vehicle), and out to Playalinda Beach.

Playalinda Beach is the most popular area of Canaveral National Seashore and almost certainly the only place in the world where you can sunbathe in full view of spacecraft launch pads. Another unpaved road, the **Max Hoeck Creek Wildlife Drive**, where you can sometimes see alligators, runs one way from Playalinda to rejoin Highway 402 near the entrance station. The beach is closed for three days before scheduled space shuttle launches.

Lodging

If it can be squeezed into your trip budget, make reservations to stay at Walt Disney World. All WDW hotels are expensive compared to similar accommodations anywhere else in Florida, but the extra money is well spent, as it makes your escape from reality complete. You'll want the room for the nights before, during, and after your Walt Disney World visit because you'll be getting up early and getting back late. For example, our suggested schedule is for a two-day visit, so we'd spend three nights (and a big chunk of our trip budget) at one of the Disney hotels; if we were traveling with children and pleasingly plump wallets, we'd probably plan to see Walt Disney World on a five-day passport and make hotel reservations for six nights.

The most lavish of the Disney-owned hotels on the Walt Disney World grounds (we mention this first so the others will seem affordable by comparison) is the **Grand Floridian Beach Resort**, an even more ornate reproduction of one of Henry Flagler's grand hotels, the Royal Poinciana (which is no longer standing) at Palm Beach. The only thing the Grand Floridian lacks is the Atlantic Ocean, but it compensates with an amazingly convincing turn-of-the-century ambience, six restaurants, views and boat rentals on Seven Seas Lagoon, and monorail service to the nearby Magic Kingdom as well as Epcot Center. Guest rooms run upward from $180 nightly in season—just before Christmas through New Year's Day and mid-February through late April. (Walt Disney World's ''in season'' hotel rates are not related to park attendance.) Off-season rates are about $15 a night less. Some suites cost $800 a night.

At the other end of the lodging spectrum, the new **Caribbean Beach Resort** is the largest hotel in Walt Disney World (over 2,000 rooms) and comes closest to offering ''budget'' accommodations (around $80 a night). Located near Epcot Center, it has shuttle bus service but no monorail service.

A quieter, much smaller Walt Disney World resort on a tropical theme is the **Polynesian Village Resort**, situated on a man-made beach on Seven Seas Lagoon south of the Grand Floridian. This hotel is popular among return visitors (who have had the opportunity to see the various options in person before making reservations) and fills up quickly, so if you want to stay here, book your room far in advance. Room rates start at $150 a night, $15 less off-season. It has monorail service.

Similar room rates to those at the Polynesian Resort can be found at the massive **Contemporary Resort**, where the monorail runs through the lobby and amenities include a 24-hour video game room as well as two swimming pools and a beach and marina on Bay Lake near the Magic Kingdom entrance. For a few dollars less, you can stay at the **Disney Inn**, formerly known as the Golf Resort. The inn's location, well removed from the monorail route and lakefront, is appreciated even by nongolfers who want a place to escape the crowds. Two golf courses adjoin the inn: the Palm (which *Golf Digest* rates among the nation's top 100 courses) to the south and the Magnolia to the north. Green fees are about $40. Shuttle buses connect the inn with the transportation center, where you can catch the monorail to Epcot Center or the Magic Kingdom.

In the eastern part of Walt Disney World, far from the Magic Kingdom but convenient to the Shopping Village, the Pleasure Island nightlife complex, River Country, and Epcot Center, are an assortment of villas that cost about $200 for a one-bedroom, $275 for a two- or three-bedroom ($20-$25 less off-season). The latter are a reasonable option for families large enough that they would otherwise rent two rooms in a hotel. The most unusual are the three-bedroom **Treehouse Villas**, elevated on stilts and hidden in the woods. Tennis courts and another golf course are nearby. In the same area as the villas are four **Grand Vista Suites**, luxury homes originally built as part of a Walt Disney World housing development that never materialized. The most spacious accommodations in the park, they rent for about $600 per night.

For reservations at any Disney-owned accommodation, contact Walt Disney World Central Reservations, Box 10100, Lake Buena Vista, FL 32830, (407) 824-8000. Reservations should be made at least 30 days in advance, and you must pay a deposit in the amount of one night's room rate within 21 days. A few rooms are often available at the last minute, and there are special procedures for making reservations on short notice using a credit card for the deposit. Check-in time is 3:00 p.m. for all Disney-owned hotels except the villas, where it is 4:00 p.m. Guests at any of the Disney-owned hotels can use resort facilities such as beaches at the other hotels. The ID card you receive when you check into any of these hotels also gives you unlimited free transportation within Walt Disney World, small discounts on admission to the parks, and charge privileges at most shops and restaurants except those in the Magic Kingdom.

There are several non-Disney hotels at the Hotel Plaza in Walt Disney World Village. They include the **Pickett Suite Resort** (800-742-5288), the **Hilton** (which offers "Youth Hotel" child care service for ages 3 to 12, 800-445-8667), the **Buena Vista Palace** (800-432-2920), the **Howard Johnson Resort** (800-654-2000), the **Hotel Royal Plaza** (800-248-7890), the **Viscount** (800-348-3765), and the **Grosvenor Resort** (800-624-4109). But try hard to stay at a Disney-owned hotel instead. Room rates are not significantly lower at Hotel Plaza (starting rates range from about $80 at Howard Johnson's and the Grosvenor to about $130 at the Hilton) and nobody does Walt Disney World accommodations as well as Disney does.

Outside Walt Disney World, there is never a shortage of accommodations in the Orlando-Kissimmee area. In fact, there are about 20,000 guest rooms around, and except during school vacation periods you can count on finding a motel with a vacancy when you arrive. The greater the distance from Walt Disney World, the lower room rates will be. (Too far away, though, it will be harder to get up in time to arrive at Walt Disney World first thing in the morning.) In Orlando, the main tourist hotel strip is International Drive, parallel to Interstate 4 and about 15 minutes from Walt Disney World. International Drive is loud and crowded with traffic, a real drawback if you're headed for Walt Disney World during morning rush hour (don't forget, nearly half of Orlando's workforce works at WDW). Motels also line US 441 between Orlando and Kissimmee and Highway 192 between Walt Disney World and Kissimmee. In any of these areas, budget motel rooms can be found for under $40 and quality accommodations for up to $150 per night. Don't expect the lush surroundings or imaginative touches that make the Disney-owned resorts so special, though. Out of "the World," motels tend to be incredibly ordinary.

Orlando's exceptional new grand hotel is the **Peabody** at 9801 International Drive (across from the Orlando/Orange County Convention Center). Call (305) 352-4000 or (800) COCONUT for reservations. The original Peabody in Memphis, Tennessee, has a long-standing reputation as the most elegant hotel in the South. The far more modern Orlando version offers the same fine amenities and service. The ambience is stately, and potted palm trees are everywhere. As in Memphis, a trained team of royal ducks parades through the lobby for their traditional daily swim in the fountain. Room rates range from $115 to $175, about the same as the cost of staying at a Walt Disney World hotel.

Camping

Walt Disney World's RV park, **Fort Wilderness Campground Resort**, is big (over 1,000 sites), pricey ($35 to $40 a night for full hookups, $29 without hookups, $4 less off-season), and worth it. Even if it weren't within Walt Disney World, Fort Wilderness would be among the finest RV resorts in the United States. It is set on 780 acres of forestland and has more recreational facilities than any of the other accommodations areas, including a 1½-mile nature trail, a beach, a marina, swimming pools, canals for boating and fishing, bicycle rentals, guided horseback rides, two game arcades, a musical review, and a campfire program featuring Disney movies and cartoons. River Country, Disney's Huck Finn-style water park (daily admission about $10), is nearby. The only drawbacks are that pets are not allowed here or anywhere else in Walt Disney World (for about

$4 per night—$6 including food—they can be boarded at the kennel at the campground entrance, near an open field where you can walk them) and advance reservations are essential (make them through Walt Disney World Central Reservations— see Lodging, above, for the address and phone number).

There are two KOA campgrounds in the Walt Disney World area: **KOA Walt Disney World East/Kissimmee**, five miles east of Walt Disney World on US 192 ($23 per night, 305-396-2400 or 800-331-1435), and **KOA Theme World**, ten miles west of Walt Disney World via Interstate 4 at the US 27 exit (across from Boardwalk and Baseball, $18 per night, 813-424-1242). There are **Yogi Bear's Jellystone Park** campgrounds in the area at 8555 West Space Coast Parkway in Kissimmee and on Turkey Lake Road in Orlando. Rates are $15 per night; for reservations at either one, call 800-327-7115. Shaded campsites (a rare commodity in central Florida RV parks) are available in a citrus orchard at the otherwise modest **Orange Grove Campground**, five miles east of Walt Disney World at 2425 Old Vineland Road, Kissimmee ($13 to $16 per night, 407-396-6655).

WALT DISNEY WORLD: EPCOT CENTER

Walt Disney World is the world's largest commercial tourist attraction. Forty-six square miles in area (twice the size of Manhattan), "the World" receives 25 million visitors a year (twice the total population of Florida) and grosses $2 billion a year. Its staff of 26,000 cast members makes Walt Disney World the largest nongovernment employer in the state.

Visit Epcot Center first. The exhibits and activities here emphasize education, not escapism as in most of the rest of the World. They are lavish, big-budget exhibits that incorporate every imaginable attention-getter, and yet . . .ask any kid, tall or small, whether he'd rather learn about energy technology or ride the Adventureland Jungle Cruise, and the answer probably won't surprise you. In short, children (and many adults, too) who visit the Magic Kingdom first may find Epcot Center anticlimactic. But if the last attraction you visited was Kennedy Space Center, you'll be in an ideal frame of mind for the state-of-the-art technological journeys found here.

Suggested Schedule

8:00 a.m.	After breakfast, head for Epcot Center.
8:30 a.m.	Be at the Epcot Center entrance when it opens.
9:00 a.m.	Bypass Spaceship Earth for now. Leave an adult member of your group at Earth Station (the exit from Spaceship Earth) to make lunch/dinner reservations while the rest of you proceed counterclockwise around the park to visit The Living Seas and The Land. Arrange to meet in the entrance line for Journey into Imagination.
10:30 a.m.	Visit World Showcase. Try to see one or more of the popular rides and theater presentations before the crowd catches up with you, then wander the foreign streets when they are busy.
3:00 p.m.	Eat a good meal at one of the World Showcase restaurants (reservations required at most of them).
5:00 p.m.	Return to Future World. See the World of Motion and other attractions on the east side of the park, as well as Spaceship Earth.
8:00 or 9:00 p.m.	Return to your accommodations after a very full day.

Walt Disney World
Our touring strategy is designed to pack as much as possible of
Walt Disney World into two days. This is nowhere near enough
time to see everything. Before its latest expansion, Walt Disney
World was designed to keep visitors fully occupied for five days;
now, with the addition of Disney-MGM Studios and Typhoon
Lagoon, seven days is more like it. If you are traveling with
preteen children, Walt Disney World will unquestionably be the
high point of their Florida odyssey; omit other destinations in
this itinerary and plan for as much time here as your trip budget
will allow. Even for childless adult travelers, Walt Disney World
deserves to be seen, and this plan will show you most of the
high points in a whirlwind visit.

Walt Disney World is the most expensive destination in this
itinerary. A family of two adults and two children over age three
staying in Walt Disney World accommodations can expect to
spend about $300 per day ($100 per day for park admission,
though you can save about 25 percent with a three-day passport or 35 percent with a five-day passport; about $140 per day
for accommodations at one of the mid-priced Disney hotels;
and at least $60 a day for meals—you're not allowed to bring
your own picnic lunch into the park).

Admission prices, which include nearly all rides and other
attractions, seem to change as often as the weather. Expect to
pay about $28 per adult and $22 per child for a one-day admission to either the Magic Kingdom or Epcot Center (substantially
less for Riverworld, Discovery Island, or Typhoon Lagoon;
prices for admission to the new Disney-MGM Studios have not
been announced as of this writing). The drawback to one-day
admissions is that you can't visit more than one of these parks
in the same day; if you have limited time but plenty of money
and a burning desire to catch at least a glimpse of everything, a
multiday World Passport, which covers all the parks, may be
just the ticket for you even though you may not plan to stay for
its duration. (Then, again, possession of one of these passports
may inspire you to stay an extra day.) Three-day passports cost
approximately $75 for adults and $55 for children; four days,
$90 for adults and $65 for children; and five days, $100 for
adults and $75 for children. Walt Disney World is considering
phasing out the three-day passports with the opening of
Disney-MGM Studios.

The secret for touring Epcot Center or the Magic Kingdom
efficiently is to arrive early and get in line for the most popular
attractions before the midday crowds build. Both parks normally open at 9:00 a.m., and if you arrive at 8:00 or 8:15 you can
enter about half an hour before the rides begin operation, plac-
ing you among the first in line for most attractions or in the run-
ning for the daily opening race to Space Mountain. During busy

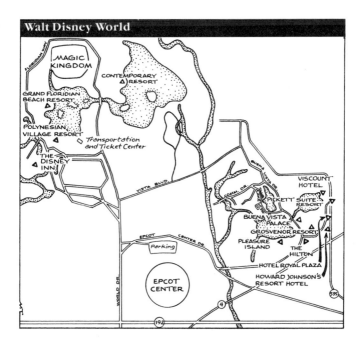

periods, which Disney computers calculate the day before based on hotel reservations, the parks may open earlier in the morning. If this is the case, you'll still want to arrive an hour before opening. To find out the exact opening time, phone (407) 824-4321 on the day before you plan to visit. Closing times vary even more. Epcot Center normally closes at 8:00 p.m. but stays open later during busy periods; the Magic Kingdom closes as early as 6:00 p.m. during slow times and stays open as late as 10:00 p.m. during the busiest periods.

The busiest times at Walt Disney World are the week between Christmas and New Year's Day (by far the most crowded time, with up to 90,000 visitors per day in each of the major parks), the Thanksgiving holidays, spring break, and the summer months from Memorial Day to Labor Day. The least crowded times are December (until Christmas) and January through mid-February. The busiest days of the week are Monday through Wednesday, and the most crowd-free day is Friday.

Epcot Center
"Epcot" was Walt Disney's acronym for Experimental Prototype Community of Tomorrow. As he originally proposed it in 1966, shortly before his death and two years before ground was broken on Walt Disney World, Epcot would have been a utopian

small city, complete with residential complexes and schools, where Disney employees could live, work, play, and serve as guinea pigs for shaping a better future.

By the time Epcot Center became a reality in 1982, its concept had changed completely. Far from becoming the twenty-first-century village Disney had envisioned, Epcot took on the attributes of a permanent World's Fair, a collection of mind-expanding adventures in high tech along with a series of international pavilions showing off the foods and cultures of eleven nations. Educational? Well, sure, but high school was never like this. Distractions such as video games or MTV wouldn't stand a chance of luring young minds away from the ideas presented here. Epcot Center is divided into two parts: Future World, which exhibits advances in science and technology, and World Showcase, with pavilions representing Canada, Great Britain, France, Morocco, Japan, Italy, Germany, China, Norway, Mexico, and, of course, the United States.

Many of the top attractions here, as well as in the Magic Kingdom and Disney-MGM Studios, rely on Audio-Animatronics, a computer-controlled robot technology developed specifically for Disneyland and Walt Disney World, so lifelike that one can't help but wonder how long before personal computers will be replaced by cute talking bears and vacuum cleaners will become Bette Midler look-alikes.

Future World Sightseeing Highlights
▲▲▲ **Spaceship Earth**—The 180-foot-high silver geosphere, which you can't miss as you enter Epcot Center, houses Audio-Animatronic exhibits that trace the development of communications from prehistoric rock art to modern computer net works. The spiraling "time tunnel" that carries you through the displays starts around 30,000 B.C. and culminates poised on the brink of the future—with a panoramic view of the universe. Science fiction author Ray Bradbury scripted the journey, based on suggestions from consultants at the Smithsonian Institution, the Huntington Library, the University of California, and the University of Chicago; AT&T paid for it.

The only times you can hope to avoid long lines at Spaceship Earth are early in the morning and during the dinner hour. Since it is the first attraction visitors encounter on entering Epcot Center, most people stop here first. If you've followed our advice and arrived early, skipping Spaceship Earth for now and seeing it when you leave this evening can give you a chance to get ahead of the crowd, be first in line for one of other Future World attractions such as The Living Seas, The Land, or Journey into Imagination, and reach the World Showcase Port of Entry before the late morning rush hour.

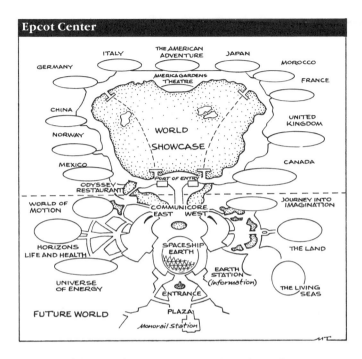

Epcot Center

ITALY
THE AMERICAN ADVENTURE
JAPAN
GERMANY
MOROCCO
AMERICA GARDENS THEATRE
FRANCE
CHINA
UNITED KINGDOM
NORWAY
WORLD
SHOWCASE
MEXICO
CANADA
PORT OF ENTRY
ODYSSEY RESTAURANT
WORLD OF MOTION
JOURNEY INTO IMAGINATION
COMMUNICORE
EAST   WEST
HORIZONS
LIFE AND HEALTH
SPACESHIP EARTH
THE LAND
UNIVERSE OF ENERGY
EARTH STATION *(information)*
ENTRANCE
THE LIVING SEAS
FUTURE WORLD
PLAZA
Monorail Station

CommuniCore—The two vast covered pavilions that surround Future World's three-tiered central fountain are packed
with exhibits, most of them about exchanging information,
many of them "hands-on" or interactive, with more TV screens
than you've ever seen in one place. You could easily spend all
morning here playing with touch-sensitive computer screens,
video telephones, talking typewriters, computerized artists, and
the like. But if your goal is to see all the best of Epcot Center on
a one-day ticket, it's best to pass by these lesser displays on your
way to the rides/pavilions that ring the perimeter of Future
World. Perhaps the most interesting of the CommuniCore
attractions is the Future Choice Theater in CommuniCore East,
where audience members participate in an opinion poll and see
instant results, complete with demographic analysis, on the theater screen. While you wait for the next seating, you can watch
a large array of TV sets showing broadcasts from around the
world. Future Choice Theater operates from 11:00 a.m. to
7:00 p.m.

▲▲**The Living Seas**—This aquarium's feature attraction is a
too-brief underwater ride that simulates a dive to a Caribbean
coral reef. While the "hydrolator" capsule you ride in actually

descends only two inches below the surface of the 5.7-million-gallon tank inhabited by 6,000 marine creatures, the deep-sea illusion is very realistic. Other Living Seas exhibits include Seabase Alpha (a full-scale model of a futuristic undersea research station), a film that explains the oceans' role in world ecology, and a mural and a multi-image show that trace the development of diving technologies. Here, too, you'll see a diving suit and large model submarine that were used to film the 1954 Disney classic, *20,000 Leagues Under the Sea*. The Living Seas outclasses the Magic Kingdom's perpetually crowded 20,000 Leagues ride even without a giant squid.

▲▲**The Land**—The largest pavilion in Future World, The Land highlights innovations predicted for twenty-first-century agriculture. On the 13-minute Listen to the Land boat ride, you'll find out how to grow crops in outer space and how to make the desert bloom; there is even a South American rain forest—fabricated entirely from polyethylene plastic. Also not to be missed is the Audio-Animatronic Kitchen Kabaret, the funniest show in Future World, in which narrator Bonnie Appetit explains nutrition with the help of lively characters (from the four basic food groups) such as a stand-up comic egg and a punk-rock broccoli stalk.

▲▲▲**Journey into Imagination**—This pavilion is housed in the double pyramid just beyond The Land. It can be very crowded, so if you're visiting on a busy day, you may wish to leave it until the early evening hours when the line is shorter. But whenever you can fit it into your Epcot Center visit, don't miss it! The 14-minute Journey into Imagination ride traces the adventures of sword-and-sorcery hero Dreamfinder and his creation/companion, a purple dragon named Figment, as they (and you) discover the many roles of imagination in art, science, and literature. Outstanding special effects help explain a fascinating subject that many schoolteachers wouldn't touch with a fork. In the same pavilion is The Image Works, a "hands-on" activity area that lets you draw with laser beams, conduct an electronic orchestra, and create colors with your voice or music with your footsteps. This one-of-a-kind playground is not only a wonderful place to unleash your right brain but also a great people-watching spot. Finally, before leaving the pavilion, don't miss *Captain Eo*, a 3-D musical space fantasy directed by Francis Ford Coppola, starring Michael Jackson and still more special effects.

▲▲▲**World of Motion**—Located in the northeast corner of Future World, this pavilion is about travel and transportation. The main ride, It's Fun to be Free, takes you along on mankind's quest for speedier ways to get from here to there, from attempts to ride ostriches to prophecies of future high-speed aerial trains. (By the way, back in the real world, plans are now under way to build the first "bullet train" in the United States between Walt Disney World and Orlando International Airport, 20 miles away.) When you exit from It's Fun to be Free, you'll pass through TransCenter, where exhibits include a robot auto assembly line and prototypes for vehicles of the future. (This pavilion is sponsored by General Motors.)

▲▲**Horizons**—The 15-minute ride that takes you through this pavilion will unify the many new technologies and ideas you've already seen in Future World. After paying homage to past futurists like Jules Verne, it reaches farther into the realm of speculation than most of the other pavilions. You visit a space colony, an undersea farm, and a floating city. A unique feature of the ride is that you and the other three passengers in your car get to choose by democratic vote how it ends.

[NEW] **Wonders of Life**—This latest addition to Future World, about the human body, is just opening as *22 Days in Florida* goes to press. It will feature Body Wars (a flight simulator ride through the human bloodstream), Cranium Wars (an Audio-Animatronic program about how brain and body interact), and—pending a final decision from the exhibit's sponsor, Metropolitan Life Insurance—perhaps a film showing the conception and birth of a human child. Now, really, can you resist seeing sex education Walt Disney-style? (Which way to the "hands-on" exhibits?)

▲▲**Universe of Energy**—Don't give up because the line in front of this pavilion looks hopeless. It's a part-ride, part-theater attraction, and 850 people will enter at the same time. Then the line won't move for nearly an hour. It's about energy, with special attention to fossil fuels (Exxon sponsors it), but the show is stolen by some very realistic dinosaurs, the largest Audio-Animatronic beasts ever built.

World Showcase
If you spend just 22 minutes in each of World Showcase's eleven "countries" and enjoy lunch at one of the many international restaurants along the way, your round-the-world tour will take a minimum of five hours. You'll linger longer in some countries and reluctantly breeze through others as you make your way around a 1¼-mile waterfront, and by the time you arrive back at the Port of Entry, you'll feel as if you'd walked from Canada to Mexico. There is public transportation—two ferries "cruise" back and forth between the Port of Entry and Germany or Morocco and buses run constantly around the lake—but we've found that waiting to board them usually takes longer than walking.

World Showcase, and each of the countries within it, is a microcosm in the truest sense. The experiences are unlike anything that you would encounter if you actually visited France, Mexico, or China, but the memories they create are much like those a militantly positive romanticist would bring back from 22-day visits to these nations. For example, the Canada pavilion packages 4,000 miles worth of sights—a Quebecois boutique, an Ottawa grand hotel replica, a Rocky Mountain, a Northwest Canada trading post, and a garden inspired by Butchart Gardens in Victoria, British Columbia—into an area about the size of a neighborhood shopping mall. The great sights of Canada that can't be contained within this reproduction are displayed in a wraparound movie shown all day inside the mountain.

In each country, Walt Disney World goes to great lengths to achieve authenticity within artifice: the goods sold in stores are imported from the respective countries (much more expensive here than there, but think what you're saving in plane fare), almost all staff personnel were born in the nations they represent, and virtually all landscaping vegetation is native to the various nations. Notice the motion picture set design technique, called "forced perspective," that has been used to make landmarks such as buildings and mountains appear really BIG by miniaturizing details of the higher parts such as upper-level windows. For example, Canada's Rocky Mountain is actually about 20 stories tall (a high elevation for Florida) but appears to reach thousands of feet into the sky; the Eiffel Tower is only 74 feet tall, about a tenth the size of the Paris original, but looks every bit as big.

World Showcase has fewer rides or theater presentations to wait in line for than are found in Epcot's Future World or the Magic Kingdom. The big attractions here (as would be the case on quick visits to the nations themselves) are restaurants, shopping, landmarks, and ambience; several of the street scenes, such as Morocco's market, are more convincing when crowded, making them the best place in Epcot Center to spend the busy midday hours. This is good camera territory, since each country offers at least one viewpoint from which it looks just like the real place—only better.

The major rides in World Showcase are El Rio del Tiempo (7 minutes) in Mexico and, even better, the Viking Maelstrom (ride and film, 14 minutes) in Norway, both to your left from the Port of Entry. The outstanding wraparound motion picture presentations are *O Canada* (18 minutes) inside Canada's mountain, *Impressions de France* (18 minutes) in France's Palais du Cinema (both to your right from the Port of Entry), and *Wonders of China* (19 minutes) inside the Temple of Heaven replica, beyond Norway. The only major Audio-Animatronics/

multimedia show is the United States' American Adventure (29 minutes), a historical reenactment so realistic—serious research went into discovering such details as tones of voice and mannerisms of people like Benjamin Franklin and Mark Twain—that on leaving, you may momentarily wonder whether the strangers around you are also cleverly computerized plastic robots. It is presented in the nearly full-scale reproduction of Liberty Hall directly across the lake from the Port of Entry. Try to visit several of these major wait-in-line attractions early and wander the streets afterward.

Food in Epcot Center

Make meal reservations as soon as you arrive at Epcot Center. Earth Station, the exit port of Spaceship Earth, is a computerized information center where you can make reservations at any of the Epcot Center restaurants. By eating a hearty breakfast before you arrive at Epcot and waiting until mid-afternoon (after 2:00) to dine there, you can avoid the most crowded times at the restaurants and see major attractions during conventional lunch and dinner hours when the lines tend to be shorter.

Each of the major World Showcase countries has at least one sit-down restaurant, and reservations are required for all of them except **Le Cellier** cafeteria in Canada. The best food and atmosphere for the price (generally about $6 to $13 per person for lunch and $10 to $20 for dinner) can be found at **Les Chefs de France** (seafood) and **Le Bistro de Paris** (Continental cuisine), both in France, **Akershus** in Norway, the **Biergarten** in Germany, and especially Mexico's **San Angel Inn**, where the Mexican food is truly Mexican, not the more familiar Americanized version. The only ''reservations required'' restaurant where you stand a chance of getting a table without reservations is **El Marrakech** in Morocco, less popular simply because most visitors are unfamiliar with Moroccan cuisine.

In Future World, the place to eat is the **Land Grille Room** in The Land (naturally enough, since food production is the subject of this pavilion sponsored by Kraft Foods). Most menu items are American, imaginative, and delicious. There is also a very popular seafood restaurant at The Living Seas, but the food quality is not exceptional; most other parts of Florida abound with outstanding seafood restaurants.

You are not allowed to bring picnic food into either Epcot Center or the Magic Kingdom. You *are* allowed to exit the park temporarily, eat in your vehicle, and return on the same ticket.

Nightlife: Pleasure Island

Epcot Center's nightly spectacular is Illuminations—fireworks and a laser light show above World Showcase Lagoon near closing time.

If you're the kind of night person who feels full of energy after the sun goes down, notwithstanding ten or twelve hours in Epcot Center, the newly opened Pleasure Island near Walt Disney World Village was designed with you in mind. The "island" is supposedly the former home of nineteenth-century ship-building tycoon Merriweather Adam Pleasure (not really, but reality is what you come to Walt Disney World to escape from, right?). There are six very different night spots on the island, all for a single admission charge. Among them are the **XZFR Rockin RollerDrome**, the **Comedy Warehouse**, the live entertainment **Neon Armadillo Saloon**, the spooky **Adventurer's Club**, and the high-tech **Videopolis**; there are also restaurants and movies.

Other evening entertainment possibilities include several dinner theater shows in Walt Disney World resorts: the **Top of the World** at the Contemporary Resort (Broadway easy listening, about $40 per person), the **Polynesian Revue** at the Polynesian Village (South Seas dancing, about $30 per person), and the **Hoop Dee Doo Revue** at Fort Wilderness (rowdy frontier dancehall show with chuck wagon-style supper, about $30). Reservations can be hard to get; the Hoop Dee Doo Review may be booked up months in advance (Fort Wilderness campers get priority on the waiting list for cancellations). If you're interested in seeing any of these shows, inquire about reservations when you check into your Walt Disney World accommodations, or if you're staying outside the World, call 824-2748 (for the Hoop Dee Doo Review) or 824-8000 (for the others) as soon after 9:00 a.m. as possible.

See the Food section in Day 5 for the top outside-the-World dinner shows in the Orlando-Kissimmee area.

WALT DISNEY WORLD: THE MAGIC KINGDOM AND BEYOND

Over the years, Walt Disney's Magic Kingdom seems to have changed by remaining the same. Adult visitors now outnumber children four to one, and for many the Magic Kingdom has become less a playground than a venerable institution, a sort of Childhood National Park where forgotten dreams wait to be relived. Whenever schools are out (spring break, all summer, Thanksgiving weekend, and especially from December 20 through January 2), the Magic Kingdom is crawling with kids, but at other times, such as early December, late January, and February, the park seems taken over by still-youngsters remembering their first Mousketeer ears or coonskin hats and humming, "Who's the leader of the club that's made for you and me? M-I-C (See you real soon) K-E-Y (Why? Because we like you!). . . ."

Suggested Schedule

8:30 a.m.	Be waiting at the Magic Kingdom when it opens. See Main Street attractions including the Walt Disney Story.
9:00 a.m.	Start in Adventureland and work your way around the park to Tomorrowland, riding all the rides that time permits. Even standing in line is fun here.
5:00 p.m.	Finally, get in line for Space Mountain.
6:00 p.m.	Ride Space Mountain.
6:05 p.m.	What a thrill that was! Want to get back in line?
Evening	Leave the park for dinner or stick around for the Main Street Electrical Parade.

The Magic Kingdom
This landmark amusement park has changed very little since 1968, two years after Walt Disney's death, when it was cloned from Disneyland in southern California (which Disney built in 1955). Since then, other Disneyland parks have gone up on the outskirts of Paris and Tokyo, but the Magic Kingdom still outshines its siblings. For example, the Magic Kingdom's Cinderella Castle is much taller than its sister Sleeping Beauty Castle in Disneyland, as is the Magic Kingdom version of Space Mountain.

The overwhelming impression of the Magic Kingdom, true all over Walt Disney World but most apparent here, is one of

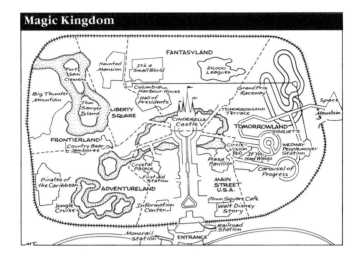

absolute orderliness. Tourist traffic meanders around the park as
smoothly as a river, and while there may be long, long lines for
the major rides, Disney planners have gone to extraordinary
lengths to distract you with ambience during the wait. Trash is
nonexistent; "cast members" are everywhere ready to pounce
on any stray bit of debris. (You can test this by tossing crumpled
paper on the sidewalk of Main Street, then watching and timing
how long before it vanishes. In our experiments, it took just
over one minute.)

Magic Kingdom Sightseeing Highlights
The Magic Kingdom has rides galore, and even when atten-
dance is relatively light, you will not have time to try them all.
Fortunately, you won't want to. Many, particularly in Fantasyland, are what used to be known as "C ticket" rides back in
the days when park admission came with a book of "A," "B,"
and "C" tickets to limit the number of star attractions you could
ride. Today, these minor rides, such as whirling teacups and
elephants that fly around in a circle, disguised versions of standard carnival rides, are primarily frequented by younger children who can't tolerate too many long waits in line. Here are the
sine qua nons for a one-day Magic Kingdom visit.
▲▲ **Main Street, U.S.A.** — The better-than-life re-creation of a
small-town American main street from Walt Disney's early-
twentieth-century boyhood opens half an hour earlier than the
rest of the park. Two Main Street attractions provide background and orientation for the first-time visitor. The **Walt Disney Story**, in the yellow building to your right as you enter the

park, is a film presentation that recounts the career of the Missouri farmboy who went on to create America's most familiar images. The **Walt Disney World Railroad**, which leaves from near the entrance gate, goes around the perimeter of the Magic Kingdom and gives you an overview of its various "lands." To keep their locations straight, note relationships to Cinderella's Castle, the entrance to Fantasyland, which is the center of the park. The castle is a third-generation fantasy: a bigger, more ornate version of Disneyland's Sleeping Beauty Castle, which in turn was patterned after Neuschwanstein Castle, built as a highly romanticized version of a medieval castle in the mid-nineteenth century by "Mad" King Ludwig II of Bavaria, who originally sponsored Wagner's operas.

▲▲▲**Space Mountain (Tomorrowland)**—This is the number one attraction in the Magic Kingdom. If you wonder whether it's worth an hour's wait in line for a ride that lasts less than three minutes, the answer is yes. Absolutely. The wait in line feels as you'd imagine it would be like in a twenty-first-century spaceport awaiting a flight to Mars or beyond. Signs warning that the ride may be hazardous to your health heighten your adrenalin level but should not scare you off. It's highly unlikely that you will have a heart attack on this ride, but you'll always carry it among your most vivid memories of Florida. What is essentially a compact, short roller-coaster ride becomes unforgettable for one reason: it's dark. Each veer and plunge comes suddenly and without warning as you hurtle among outer-space special effects. Though it lasts only two minutes and 38 seconds, it seems like light-years.

A lot of people, mostly (but not all) teenagers, visit the Magic Kingdom only to ride Space Mountain over and over. As soon as the park opens in the morning, there is a race to get in line. You can't beat the crowd here, so save Space Mountain as the climax to your visit and resolve yourself to the long wait. Instead, tour the Magic Kingdom clockwise, beginning with Adventureland.

▲▲▲**Jungle Cruise (Adventureland)**—This ride is a true classic, a replica of the jungle boat trip that was the ultimate experience in California's Disneyland when it first opened over 30 years ago. What made it special then, and still does, is the lifelike robotic African animals. What children don't notice is the remarkable number of plant species that thrive in this postage stamp of a rain forest, ranking it high among Florida's many commercial garden attractions. Shooting at hippopotamuses and fleeing from spear-brandishing Third World people may seem like unsavory thrills to some adults, but it's historic. Remember when you daydreamed about riding this boat?

▲▲**Pirates of the Caribbean (Adventureland)**—This fairly tame boat ride takes you past dioramas with some of Walt Disney World's most lifelike robotic people and animals. Though the plot is actually pretty bloodthirsty (in a G-rated way), this seven-and-a-half-minute adventure may fire your imagination for the Florida Keys (Days 10-12), where such things used to happen all the time.

▲**Country Bear Jamboree (Frontierland)**—This 15-minute musical stage show featuring some of Walt Disney World's best Audio-Animatronic characters is the most delightful sit-down-and-watch show in the Magic Kingdom. Get there early or expect to wait.

▲▲**Big Thunder Mountain Railroad (Frontierland)**—A three-minute, half-mile plunge via runaway train, this ride is far less white-knuckle thrilling than Space Mountain on the other side of the park, but the scenery is worth it. The 197-foot "mountain" modeled after rugged northeastern Arizona geology is so out of place in flat Florida (Big Thunder Mountain is within about 100 feet of the highest elevation in the state), where bare rock is hardly ever seen, that its escapism value is unsurpassed.

▲▲▲**Haunted Mansion (Liberty Square)**—The mansion's exterior is fabulous. A replica of an eighteenth-century Dutch estate house along the Hudson River, it rivals even Cinderella's Castle as a masterpiece of artificial architecture. Inside, the convincing spook ride shows off Walt Disney World's best array of special-effects holograms (3-D images made using a laser-photography process). A ghost that appears on the seat beside you will blur the line between modern technology and magic. The tongue-in-cheek scenario helps keep this ride from being too scary for small children.

▲▲**Hall of Presidents (Liberty Square)**—This 23-minute theater presentation features a speech by Abraham Lincoln and a roll call of all 39 past U.S. presidents (George Bush will take his place in the assembly by the end of 1989). The presidents are all Audio-Animatronic robots. Meticulous research went into creating their realistic mannerisms, speaking voices, and period dress. It's worth waiting in line for, but if time constraints mean choosing between this and the American Adventure show in Epcot Center's World Showcase, the Epcot rendition of American history is by far the better choice.

▲**It's a Small World (Fantasyland)**—This 11-minute boat ride around a world-in-miniature inhabited by singing, dancing dolls, originally created for the 1964 New York World's Fair, is a must-see for younger children. Adults may find the wide-eyed celebration of international brotherhood too syrupy-sweet, a letdown after visiting the life-size microcosm of Epcot Center's World Showcase. Warning: The simple, catchy theme song is likely to rattle around in your head for the rest of your vacation.

▲ **20,000 Leagues under the Sea (Fantasyland)**—Long, long lines attest to the perennial popularity of this underwater ride, but we suggest that you be satisfied with the Living Sea trip in Epcot Center for now, look forward to the real thing at John Pennekamp Coral Reef State Park (Day 10), and get your giant squid thrills later by renting the original 1954 Disney classic from the kid-vid section of your local video store.

Skyway—The aerial tramway between Fantasyland and Tomorrowland offers a view of the Magic Kingdom from above. Considering the wait in line, it's slower than walking—but more fun.

WEDway PeopleMover (Tomorrowland)—The small train that loads near the StarJets ride and takes you on a ten-minute tour of Tomorrowland was originally a prototype for a public transit system that has never yet been used in the "real world." It proves not only that pollution-free, low-cost urban transportation is possible but that it was possible in 1971, when energy crises were still in the future.

[NEW] **Dreamflight (Tomorrowland)**—Sponsored by Delta Airlines, this short (4½-minute) ride makes you feel like you're flying as it shows you the history and future of manned flight. A new attraction for 1989, it has been overshadowed by bigger projects in the current billion-dollar Walt Disney World expansion; relatively unknown and unnoticed, Dreamflight can often be seen without waiting long in line.

▲▲ **American Journeys (Tomorrowland)**—This fascinating travelogue takes you all around the United States in 21 minutes. The film, shown on a 360-degree wraparound projection screen 270 feet in circumference, uses masterful aerial and underwater photography to zoom you through Glacier Bay in Alaska, Mount St. Helens in Washington (filmed just days after the volcano erupted), Dodger Stadium in Los Angeles, and Monument Valley in Arizona. Surfing in Hawaii, white water rafting in the Grand Canyon, and a space shuttle lift-off at Kennedy Space Center are among the thrills.

▲ **Mission to Mars (Tomorrowland)**—This is an updated version of another childhood memory, the original spaceship ride that was the feature Tomorrowland attraction when Disneyland opened in the 1950s. Back then, before the dawn of the space program, when satellites were still a science fiction dream, it was Disney's boldest foray into the future. Today, the spaceship simulation seems as quaint as a Jules Verne submarine, but new film keeps it alive and exciting. The trip now uses NASA footage from the unmanned Mariner expeditions to Mars to show you Olympus Mons (the tallest known mountain, three times as high as Mount Everest) and Valles Marineris (the deepest known can-

yon, more than twice the depth of the Grand Canyon). Special
effects are fine, but these views of the landscape on a distant
planet are the real thing. Seeing them in the context of a pre-
space-age ride can be a vivid reminder of how far mankind has
traveled in our lifetime.

▲▲ **Main Street Electrical Parade**—This extravaganza takes
place nightly at 9:00, just before the Magic Kingdom closes. (At
busy times of year, when the park stays open late, it is repeated
at 11:00 p.m.) The best place to watch is from the railroad depot,
though anywhere along Main Street will do. It features two
dozen floats, 100 performers, one million electric lights, and
$30,000 worth of fireworks each night—a sparkling exclama-
tion point to punctuate your Magic Kingdom visit.

Disney-MGM Studio Tour

Until 1988, seeing the best of Walt Disney World was easy:
Epcot Center one day, the Magic Kingdom the other. But with
the opening of Disney-MGM Studios Florida, two-day visitors
face a more difficult range of choices. Skip the Magic Kingdom?
Spend an extra day and another big chunk of your trip budget?
Disney-MGM Studios is simply not to be missed.

Despite the name, Disney and MGM are not partners. Walt
Disney World bought rights from MGM to incorporate scenes
and characters from several old and new MGM movies, including *The Wizard of Oz, Casablanca, Tarzan, Alien, Raiders of
the Lost Ark*, and *Down and Out in Beverly Hills*, into its
42-minute Great Movie Ride (the longest-lasting ride attraction
in Walt Disney World). The studio tour may have been con-
ceived in response to rival Universal Studios Florida, planned to
open in spring 1990 just three miles down the highway from
Walt Disney World; or, as Disney spokesmen claim, they may
have thought of the idea first but kept it a secret. Whichever,
this journey into the workings and history of the motion picture
industry cost $300 million to create and is worth every penny;
no studio tour in Hollywood can hold a candle to it. The Audio-
Animatronic movie stars are every bit as convincing as the presidents in the Magic Kingdom or the dinosaurs in Epcot Center.
Designers here studied miles of film to capture every nuance.

Besides the Great Movie Ride, the studio tour features a stunt
theater, an audience-participation TV production, a sound
effects stage, restaurants decorated to look like movie sets, and
even real, working motion picture and animation studios where
many Disney productions are now made. The studio's
entrance/exit and commercial zone is a re-creation of Hollywood Boulevard as it appeared fifty years ago, complete with its
own Chinese Theater.

In 1990, Disney-MGM Studios will add Star Tours, the tongue-in-cheek special effects outer space trip that is already one of the top attractions at Disneyland in southern California.

While Disney-MGM Studios occupies as large an area as the Magic Kingdom (about half the size of Epcot Center), you'd have to linger and loiter to spend a whole day there. Unless you have a multiday World Passport (which would let you spend an extra few hours in Epcot Center or the Magic Kingdom), the best plan might be to relax after the tour and take advantage of some of the Walt Disney World resort facilities such as boating or beaching. If you're not staying at a Disney-owned hotel, maybe now's the time to visit the new Typhoon Lagoon, a large, lavishly landscaped water park where features include 300-foot slides, the world's largest surf-making machine, and a shipwreck.

Food

The Magic Kingdom makes no attempt to match the array of restaurant choices found at Epcot Center. In fact, most Magic Kingdom visitors subsist on the hot dogs, hamburgers, french fries, cookies, and ice cream available from fast-food vendors everywhere you look. Eat a big breakfast before you go. For a full meal in the Magic Kingdom, try the **Crystal Palace** cafeteria at the end of Main Street or the **Liberty Tree Tavern** on Liberty Square. Neither requires reservations; lines are shortest before 11:00 a.m. and between 2:00 and 5:00 p.m.

A reasonable sit-down dining option during a Magic Kingdom visit is to leave the park and ride the monorail to eat at one of the casual restaurants in the nearby resort hotels. Good bets are the **Southernaire** in the Grand Floridian, the **Coral Isle Cafe** in the Polynesian Village, and the **Terrace Buffeteria** in the Contemporary Resort.

Or you could simply snack your way through the Magic Kingdom and later leave Walt Disney World to feast at one of the many fantasy theme restaurants and dinner theaters that have sprung up around "the World's" outskirts. The most spectacular are two shows in Kissimmee that feature costumes, pageantry, and lots of horses (Kissimmee was cowboy country before the tourists came): **Arabian Nights** on US 192 just on the other side of the interstate from Walt Disney World (call 239-9223 for information and reservations) and **Medieval Times** about six miles farther east on US 192 (396-1518). Dinner and the show at either place cost about $25 per person.

CENTRAL FLORIDA

From Walt Disney World, it's possible to reach Palm Beach in
about three hours by turnpike. But if you do that, you'll miss
your chance to sniff the sweet scent of orange groves. Instead,
our suggested back road route through central Florida provides
an uncrowded all-day escape from tourist attractions.

Suggested Schedule

9:00 a.m.	Leave Walt Disney World.
4:00 p.m.	Arrive in Palm Beach. Check into your accommodations or continue to Lake Worth, keeping an eye out for "Vacancy" signs.
	Spend the night in the vicinity of Palm Beach, Lake Worth, or West Palm Beach.

Travel Route: Disney World to Palm Beach (233 miles)
From the intersection of US 192 and Interstate 4, follow I-4
south for 10 miles to the Haines City exit (US 27). Then take US
27 south for 9 congested miles to Haines City (this short segment will show you why we've decided to direct you off the
main highway on a series of scenic side roads for the rest of
today's drive).

Turn left in the center of Haines City; after about a mile, watch
for the sign marking Alternate 27 and turn right (south). Stay on
Alternate 27 for about 40 miles as the little road meanders
among orange groves, lakes, small towns like Lake Wales, and
even smaller towns like Frostproof. Rejoin US 27 a few miles
past Frostproof and follow it for about 22 miles, skirting Avon
Park and Sebring.

When you've passed Sebring, watch for US 98 and turn left
(east). Follow US 98 for 23 miles, through lazy, rhyming little
Lorida, Florida, to the junction with County Road 721. Turn
right (south).

After about 10 straight miles, County Road 721 meets Highway 70. Turn right (west), go about 3 miles to Brighton, and
then turn left (south) to find yourself back on County Road 721.
Continue on County Road 721 for 16 miles, through the center
of the Brighton Seminole Indian Reservation. Soon after you
pass the two small Seminole arts and crafts shops near the
southern reservation boundary, you'll reach Highway 78. Turn
right (west/south) and continue for 13 miles to Moore Haven
where, once more, you'll join US 27. Turn left (east) and follow

Central Florida

US 27 for 35 miles to South Bay. From there, follow Highway 80 (which is joined by US 441 and, later, US 98) for 52 miles to Palm Beach.

(The scenic route described above takes a full day at a leisurely pace. You can cut the driving time to under three hours and avoid all that peace and quiet by taking Florida's Turnpike, four exits north of the Disney World exits on I-4, for 159 high-speed miles to West Palm Beach. The toll is $5.90.)

Sightseeing Highlights
▲**Boardwalk and Baseball**—At the intersection of Interstate 4 and US 27, the baseball stadium used in spring training by the Kansas City Royals doubles as an old-fashioned amusement park with 30 rides including a ferris wheel and a wooden roller coaster. Hours are daily from 9:00 a.m. to 10:00 p.m. (until midnight on weekend evenings). Admission is $16.95 for adults, $12.95 for senior citizens and children ages 3 to 7.
▲**Brighton Seminole Indian Reservation**—The Seminole people (their name means "free people" in the Muskogee language) are descendants of Native Americans who left Georgia in the nineteenth century and runaway slaves who joined them. The U.S. Cavalry tried to relocate or otherwise "eliminate" the

Florida Seminoles in two long wars. The effort took more than 20 years (1834-1856), cost $40 million and thousands of lives, and failed. The Seminoles like to point out that they are the only Indian tribe that has never signed a peace treaty with the United States. Though still technically at war, they have never been involved in a single hostile incident since slavery was abolished.

Osceola, the man whose portrait appears on signs in front of Seminole arts and crafts shops, was the hero and martyr of the Seminole Wars. For refusing to sign a treaty that would have relocated his people to Arkansas, he was repeatedly imprisoned by the U.S. Army and eventually died in jail, hardening his people's resolve to live free or die.

The craft for which the Seminoles are best known is patchwork sewing. In their shops, you'll find many beautiful examples, from pot holders to jackets, which make great Florida souvenirs.

▲**Lake Okeechobee**—On your left for 50 miles, from the Brighton Reservation to Belle Glade, is the largest lake in Florida, the water supply for the Palm Beaches, the Gold Coast, and Miami. Even if seeing is believing, this lake is hard to believe. You can't see it at all unless you rent a boat or climb to the top of the dike that was built after a devastating 1935 hurricane blew the water out of the Lake Okeechobee and flooded all the way to Tampa Bay.

Lodging
Palm Beach accommodations are costly. Besides **The Breakers** (see tomorrow's sightseeing suggestions), laps of luxury include the historic (c. 1926) **Palm Court Hotel**, 363 Cocoanut Row, (305) 659-5800, and the **Brazilian Court**, 301 Australian Avenue, (305) 655-7740. A room at either of these hotels will cost between $150 and $200 a night.

Thrifty travelers will find motel units in the $50 to $60 range about seven miles to the south in Lake Worth. Try the **Lago Motor Inn**, 714 South Dixie Highway, (305) 585-5246, or the **White Manor Hotel**, 1618 South Federal Highway, (305) 582-7437.

Camping
The camping outlook is somewhat bleak in the Palm Beach area. Check out the large **John Prince Park Campground** on Congress Avenue in Lake Worth, where amenities include nature trails and canoe rentals. Sites cost about $15 a night. At Juno Beach, 11 miles north of Palm Beach, is the kids-oriented **Yogi-by-the-Sea Jellystone Park** campground, 1745 US 1,

(407) 622-7500, $24 a night. Camping possibilities are even fewer and farther between as you go south along the Gold Coast.

Fifteen miles off our suggested travel route to Palm Beach, about 60 miles inland on the shore of Lake Okeechobee, is **Pahokee Campground** at the state recreation area near US 441. Sites cost about $10 a night.

Food

If it's Palm Beach elegance you're after, you'll find it at **L'Auberge de France** in the Palm Court Hotel, 659-5858. Dinner here can easily run $50 per person, but luncheons cost under $15. Hours are daily from 7:00 a.m. to 11:00 a.m., 12:00 noon to 2:00 p.m., and 6:00 p.m. to 9:30 p.m. (no breakfast hours on Sundays). A Palm Beach landmark since 1921 is **Testa's Restaurant** at 221 Royal Poinciana Way, 832-0992. The menu includes steaks, seafood, and Italian dinners ranging in price from about $10 to $20.

PALM BEACH AND THE GOLD COAST

Driving around Palm Beach, the wealthiest of Florida's beach resort cities, you'll see fabulous mansions including Henry Flagler's (which you can tour) and John Lennon's (which you can't). Later, drive down the coast to Miami Beach. We suggest that you forget about the seashore route and take the interstate, as local residents do. (If you must see the Gold Coast, the 80-mile-long wall of rectangular, seemingly identical high-rise resort hotels and condominiums that hide the ocean from view, take congested Highway A1A. Don't say we didn't warn you.)

Suggested Schedule

9:00 a.m.	Drive around Palm Beach.
10:00 a.m.	Visit Whitehall, Henry Flagler's mansion turned art museum.
12:00 noon	Window-shop on Worth Avenue, one of the world's most expensive shopping districts. Perhaps stop for lunch at a sidewalk café and watch people so rich that they can actually afford to buy something in these stores.
1:30 p.m.	Drive to Miami Beach.
4:00 p.m.	Check into your Art Deco hotel for two nights.

Sightseeing in Palm Beach
In the early 1890s, the southern terminus of Henry Flagler's railroad was on the shore of Lake Worth, the part of the Inland Waterway that divided the mainland from a slender strip of barrier island covered with thousands of coconut palms, which had grown from 20,000 coconuts shipwrecked here along with a crew of Spanish sailors in 1878. Flagler set about turning the island into the most exclusive resort the world had ever seen, one that would not only rival but surpass the Riviera (thus the preponderance of Mediterranean architecture). Here he built the greatest of his hotels, the Royal Poinciana, which immediately became the new winter mecca of the super-rich. Rockefellers, Astors, Vanderbilts, and Morgans, as well as European royalty, flocked to Palm Beach for the social season. The Royal Poinciana is no longer standing, but Palm Beach remains one of the wealthiest neighborhoods on earth, thanks in part to a growing influx of wealthy French and German patrons. As you drive along mansion-lined Ocean Boulevard, you may notice a

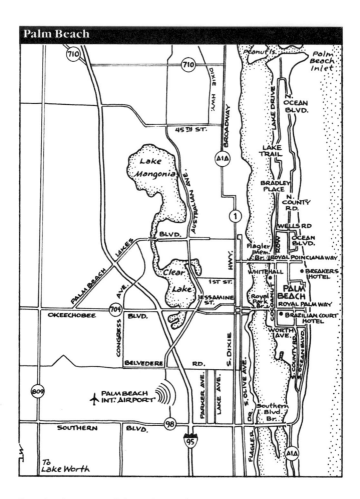

fact that has moved the rich and famous to carry protest signs: the completion of the new Palm Beach International Airport has put the world's most expensive real estate on a jetliner approach path. (Maybe money can't buy happiness after all.)

Approaching the coast on US 98, you'll cross from West Palm Beach to the "real" Palm Beach via the Southern Boulevard Bridge. Just past the Moorish, magnificent Mar-a-Lago, the largest mansion on the island (built by the heiress to the Post Toasties fortune), Southern Boulevard turns left and becomes South Ocean Boulevard, which takes you past a home that belonged to John Lennon (702 S. Ocean Blvd.) and the public beach. Turn left onto Worth Avenue, one of the world's most exclusive shopping districts. Turn right on Cocoanut Row to Whitehall.

Whitehall, the mansion Henry Flagler built for his wife in 1901 at a cost of $4 million and lived in for the final 12 years of his life, astonishes all who enter with its unabashed opulence. It was a resort hotel for over 30 years, but in 1960, after restoration, Whitehall was reopened as the **Henry Morrison Flagler Museum**. The museum contains collections of porcelain, silver, lace, and such, but the mansion itself upstages all else. Also on the grounds is Flagler's private railway car, the *Rambler*. Imagine traveling in such style. Whitehall is open Tuesday through Saturday from 10:00 a.m. to 5:00 p.m., Sundays from 1:00 p.m. to 5:00 p.m., closed Mondays. Admission is $3.50 for adults, $1.25 for children ages 6 to 12.

When you leave Whitehall, to make a circuit of the island and see still more mansions (or at least their privacy hedges), follow Cocoanut Row north as it changes names—Bradley Place, then Lake Trail, then Lake Drive. When you reach Palm Beach Inlet, the end of the island, follow North Ocean Boulevard back south to The Breakers, the finest resort hotel on Palm Beach. Be bold and stroll through the lobby. Room rates here start around $275 a night in season and go way up. (If you're interested, call 305-655-6611 or 800-833-3141 to discuss it with them. By the way, rooms here start at under $100 in the summertime.)

After another wishful thinking cruise down Worth Avenue, take the Royal Park Bridge back to the mainland and Interstate 95.

Travel Route: Palm Beach to Miami (78 miles)

Return to Interstate 95 and drive to Miami Beach the easy way. If you'd like to see a little bit of the Gold Coast without enduring the endless traffic hassles of Highway A1A all the way to Miami, exit the interstate at SW 24th Street in Fort Lauderdale. This city used to be the most popular spring break gathering place for college students and still attracts some, though Daytona is far more popular these days. The most interesting sight in Fort Lauderdale is the huge Bahia Mar marina. Mystery story fans, walk around the marina and look for Travis McGee's houseboat, the *Busted Flush*. You're not likely to find it (McGee, the hero of two dozen best-selling crime novels, is fictional and so is his boat; author John D. McDonald lives in Sarasota—Day 16), but you'll have fun searching for it. You're free to walk among the boats in practically any marina in Florida, and if you ask a question or two, you'll find that owners, captains, and crews are a friendly lot who love to talk to curious passersby. Besides the marina, Fort Lauderdale has the biggest "sin strip" on the Gold

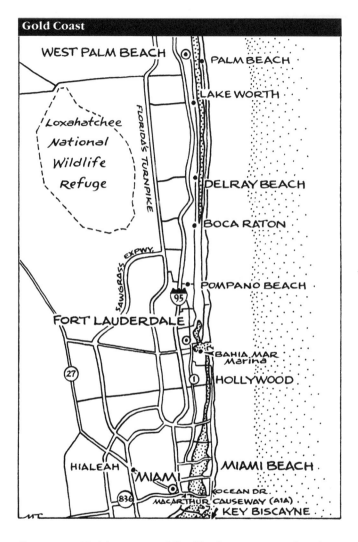

Coast—wet T-shirt contests, Miss Cheeks contests, swimsuit
contests, and stripteasers of all genders. Walt Disney World it
isn't.

Interstate 95 is the fastest way to enter Miami. If you plan to
stay in Miami Beach's Deco District (and you should unless
you're traveling on a splurge budget), get there by following
I-95 south to Highway 836 and then go east. Highway 836

becomes the MacArthur Causeway, which takes you across the
turquoise waters of Biscayne Bay, where you can glimpse private islands with elegant homes, each with a boat in its back-
yard. The last one, Star Island, has been occupied by such nota-
ble characters as Al Capone as well as a Saudi prince famed for
bouncing checks and the Ethiopian Zionist Church, whose
leader was arrested for smuggling bales of marijuana (their religious beliefs involved smoking pot all day).

On reaching Miami Beach, the MacArthur Causeway becomes
Fifth Street. Follow Fifth Street to its end, which is Ocean Drive,
and turn left. Many of our hotel recommendations are between
Fifth and Fifteenth streets on Ocean Drive.

(Travelers who have braved the traffic of Highway A1A all the
way to Miami Beach should follow it south to Fifth Street. Go
one block east and you are on Ocean Drive.)

Parking on Ocean Drive is a hassle. You must feed the meters
every two hours from 8:00 a.m. to 6:00 p.m. The ever-alert
Miami Beach police start writing a parking ticket promptly
when a meter runs out. Free parking is available three blocks
inland, but if you park on a side street, bring all your valuables
to your hotel. In fact, don't leave *anything* inside your car, even
worthless items, or they'll probably be gone when you return.
Lock everything that isn't worth carrying to your hotel room in
the car trunk. Car break-ins are epidemic. Miami Beach is not to
be missed, but precautions about car break-ins are not to be
taken lightly!

One solution to the theft problem is storing your car at All-
right Parking, 150 S.E. Second Avenue in downtown Miami, for
a fee of $6.50 per day or $25 per week, and relying on public
transportation during your visit. Another solution is to stay at a
hotel with its own parking lot, such as the Quality Inn/Gover-
nor Hotel.

If you are traveling by motor home, and you leave it on the
street unattended, it's a sitting duck. Stay at one of the Miami
area KOA campgrounds or at the Quality Inn, or store your RV
at Miami International Airport Parking Area #6 for $6 a day.
From the airport, you can take the Red Top airport shuttle to
Miami Beach for $8, or you can take Metrobus J to downtown
Miami and then change to bus A, C, or K for Miami Beach.

Lodging in Miami Beach

We recommend staying in Miami Beach's Deco District, a pastel-
colored fantasyland of quaint buildings from the 1930s and
1940s. Here's a generous sampling of possibilities.

A very original, inexpensive place to stay is the **Leonard
Beach Hotel** at 54 Ocean Drive in Miami Beach (five blocks
south of Fifth Street). Small and funky, it has a courtyard and

needs a paint job. Speaking of paint, whether or not you choose to spend the night here, stop in and ask to see one or more of the "artist rooms." The hotel flew several artists down from New York and gave each of them the opportunity to create a work of art out of one room. Each "artist room" has a story of its own, which the hotel management will be glad to tell you. One is a navy blue undersea creation with glow-in-the-dark plants; another resembles an ancient Egyptian tomb; the red-and-black "brothel" room is a fun choice for couples. The hotel also has some plain, simple rooms. Winter rates are $25 for a plain room and $30 for an "artist room"; off-season rates are $20 and $25. Some rooms have telephones, for which a $50 deposit is required. For reservations, call (305) 532-2412.

A moderate-priced hotel choice is the **Quality Inn/Governor Hotel** at 435 21st Street, two blocks west of Highway A1A. It is a beautifully renovated Art Deco hotel located in the "Museum District." Cultural amenities such as the Bass Art Museum, the Theater of the Performing Arts, and a major new convention center surround the hotel, and added features include a swimming pool, a lobby bar, and a private parking lot. Winter rates, mid-December to mid-April, range from $65 to $75 per night (as low as $40 in the "summer," mid-April to mid-December). For reservations, call (305) 532-2100.

Several small, picturesque Art Deco hotels line Ocean Drive (the place to be on Miami Beach because of its active day- and nightlife and, of course, the beach). Check out the **Waldorf Towers** at 860 Ocean Drive, (305) 531-7684 or (800) 237-3522. Winter rates range from $75 for a standard room to $150 for an oceanfront suite (summer rates are $50 to $100). The **Bentley Hotel** at 510 Ocean Drive, (305) 538-1700 or (305) 534-9703, has the same rates all year: standard rooms for $39.99, ocean-front rooms with kitchens for $60, and suites for $75. There are three **Adrian Hotels**, at 1060, 1036, and 1052 Ocean Drive. The reservation phone for all three buildings is (800) DECOTEL (that is, 332-6835). Winter rates are $50 to $70, with off-season rates as low as $35. A very popular bar featuring live music on weekends is in the lobby of the 1060 Adrian, so if you don't enjoy lots of noise, choose one of the other buildings. Another attractive Art Deco hotel, with continental breakfast, is the **Avalon**, 700 Ocean Drive, (305) 538-0133. Winter rates are $65 to $85, off-season $45 to $65.

The **Park Central Hotel**, at 640 Ocean Drive, brings a bit of Soho to Miami. Tony Goldman, one of New York's innovators of trendy chic, brought some of his style down to Miami Beach for the Park Central and other local renovations. Continental breakfast is included in the room rate, and there are a bar and a gourmet restaurant in the lobby. Winter rates are $60 for a standard

room and $165 for the best oceanfront suite; off-season rates
are $45 to $150. For reservations, call (305) 538-1611 or (800)
533-3997.

A secluded hideaway is the **Europe Guest House**, a charm-
ing, little-known bed and breakfast inn located on a residential
side street six blocks from the beach at 721 Michigan Avenue.
They have a lush garden sitting area, a Jacuzzi, and several pet
cats. Rates are $39 per night with a shared bath or $49 with a
private bath. Reservations are essential. Call (305) 538-0110. To
get there, take Fifth Street to Michigan Avenue and head north.

The **International Youth Hostel** is at 1438 Washington Avenue on Miami Beach, (305) 534-2988. Single rooms with a
shared bath cost $20, with private bath $25, double rooms $30.
To bunk down in a dormitory room with several other people,
rates are $9 for members and $11 for nonmembers. To get there,
take Highway 836 east until it turns into Fifth Street, then turn
left on Washington Avenue and go north for ten blocks.

Lodging Away from Miami Beach

Those with lots of money to spend who are willing to forsake
beaches for the glitzy jetset hangout of Coconut Grove might
consider the pyramid-shaped **Grand Bay Hotel**, 2669 South
Bayshore Drive, (305) 858-9600. The top of the pyramid houses
Miami's most prestigious nightclub, Regine's. Prices range from
$135 per night for a single room to $800 for the penthouse suite.
To get there, take I-95 South to Highway 836 West and exit at
27th Avenue South. Take 27th Avenue to the end, which is
Bayshore Drive, and turn left. Also in Coconut Grove is the
Mutiny Hotel, 2951 South Bayshore Drive, (305) 442-2400.
Each room is decorated in a different theme—the Peacock
Room, the Japanese Room, and so on. Rates run from $85 for a
standard guest room to $145 for one with a hot tub.

For a more subdued but elegant atmosphere, go to nearby
Coral Gables. The **Hyatt**, on 50 Alhambra Plaza, (305)
441-1234, looks like a grand old hotel, but it is actually one of
Miami's newest and most popular hotels. The interior is decorated in Moorish motifs. Strolling Paraguayan folk musicians ser-
enade you in the dining room, which is adjacent to the Alcazaba
Disco. On the fifth floor, a swimming pool and Jacuzzi overlook
the city of Coral Gables. Weekend rates are $130 single and $140
double; from Sunday through Thursday, prices go up to $170
and $190. To get there, take I-95 south to 836 West, exit onto
37th Avenue and go south. Turn right on Alhambra Plaza, 11
blocks south of S.W. Eighth Street. For genuine antiquity (c.
1926), the **Biltmore Hotel** has Mediterranean architecture and
the largest swimming pool in the United States. It is located at
1200 Anastasia Avenue, Coral Gables, (305) 445-1926. To get

there, exit at 37th Avenue, head south to Coral Way, turn right to Ponce de Leon, then left to Anastasia, where you turn right. Rooms range from $140 single to $175 deluxe. The **Hotel St. Michel**, 162 Alcazar Avenue, (305) 444-1666, is a tiny, pie-shaped building in downtown Coral Gables. The rooms are furnished and decorated with antiques, and they have a fancy French restaurant in the lobby. Rates are $90 for one room and $125 for a suite. To get there, take 37th Avenue south to Alhambra Plaza, turn right to Ponce de Leon, where you turn right again.

Camping

Miami has two KOA campgrounds. Neither is near major attractions, but **KOA Miami North** at 14075 Biscayne Boulevard, (305) 940-4141, is nearest to the beaches, and **KOA Miami South** at 20675 S.W. 162nd Avenue, (305) 233-5300 is closer to the Everglades National Park entrance. Sites cost about $22 a night at Miami North and $23 a night at Miami South.

MIAMI BEACH

In 1896, Henry Flagler's railroad reached the shoreline of Biscayne Bay. There, his workers hacked away the tangle of mangroves, replaced them with sand, and created the nucleus of what has become perhaps America's most remarkable urban beachfront community. Part resort, part art district, part slum, all exciting, Miami Beach is like no other place on earth. Experience it.

Suggested Schedule

10:00 a.m.	Spend the morning on the beach.
12:30 p.m.	Lunch at the News Café or Puerto Sagua.
1:30 p.m.	Take a leisurely walk to Lincoln Road, checking out nooks and crannies (where you will discover many strange and exotic things) along the way.
4:30 p.m.	South Point.
Evening	After dinner, stroll along Ocean Drive.
Later	Sample the nightlife of Old Miami Beach.

Miami Beach
Miami Beach is a long island on the east side of the city of Miami. South Beach, also known as Old Miami Beach, is the most interesting area for visitors because it oozes with character and everything is accessible on foot. Here you'll find the world's largest collection of tropical Art Deco architecture—small, fantasylike, pastel-painted buildings with curved corners, round windows, etched glass, ledges leading nowhere, and decorative friezes. Much of the neighborhood has been designated a National Historic Area.

Old Miami Beach is a popular destination for European travelers. It has also been used as a location for innumerable TV commercials, magazine layouts, films, and, of course, *Miami Vice.* Fashion models are commonly seen on streets that are closed off for media "shoots." Cheap rents and an easygoing, supportive atmosphere have made Old Miami Beach a haven for artists. This is a city to have fun in, so aside from the beach, you have a wide variety of restaurants, cafés, and nightlife to choose from. Local boutiques and vintage shops can outfit you in outrageous going-out attire.

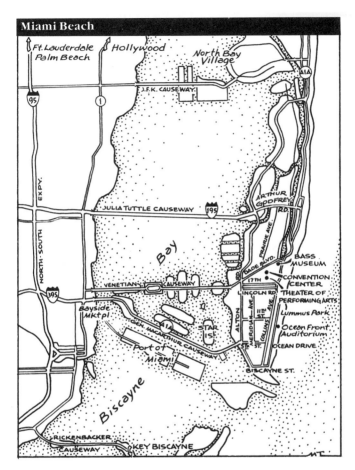

Sightseeing Highlights

▲▲▲ **Ocean Drive**—The first place to go in Miami Beach is the ten-block stretch of Ocean Drive between Fifth and Fifteenth streets, lined along the west with old hotels, distinctively "Tropical Deco" in their architecture, renovated to various levels of trendy chic. Among the cotton candy colors and creative lighting effects are sidewalk cafés and restaurants. Notice the Amsterdam Palace apartment building at 1116 Ocean Drive—a Mediterranean-style copy of Christopher Columbus's house. Across the street is Lummis Park, where a pastel-painted walkway leads you through palm and seagrape trees alongside the beach. If you hear funny noises above, look carefully among the palm fronds to catch sight of the wild green parrots that make their home there.

▲▲▲**The Beach**—Step through one of the gaps in the seawall and you're on Miami Beach. It is now very wide and white, thanks to the U.S. Army Corps of Engineers who spent a year dredging seashells from the ocean floor, grinding them up in a big machine, and spewing the result out as sand. For more safety in the event of a hurricane, they had to widen the beach. Now it is very wide, with a hill in the middle. (Before 1980, South Miami Beach was a narrow stretch of soft beige sand, which you can still wiggle your toes in near the seawall.)

Vacationers come from all over the world, so expect to hear a variety of languages and see all sorts of bathing attire. A hot local issue is toplessness, practiced by European women who are accustomed to the Riviera. It's illegal, but this is Miami Beach, and such crimes are acceptable to many.

▲▲▲**Art Deco District**—The Miami Design Preservation League Welcome Center, located two blocks inland at 661 Washington Avenue, is open Monday through Saturday from 10:00 a.m. to 6:00 p.m. and Sundays 12:00 noon to 5:00 p.m.

Until the early 1980s, Old Miami Beach went unnoticed. It was the kind of neighborhood most people locked their car doors before venturing into. One of the few people who recognized its beauty was Barbara Capitman. Through tireless effort, she and her son, Andrew, organized the Miami Design Preservation League, won National Historic District status for the neighborhood, got the preservation/restoration ball rolling, and saved Old Miami Beach from soon decaying out of existence. Very informative walking tours leave the welcome center every Saturday at 10:30 a.m. and cost $5. The welcome center also sells Art Deco books, postcards, and calendars. For everything you ever wanted to know about Deco, get a copy of the $6 *Miami Beach Art Deco Guide.*

▲▲**Deco Shopping**—Old Miami Beach shopping is. . . well. . . not like elsewhere. As you walk around the neighborhood, you're sure to see Deco-styled posters by local artist Woody Vondracheck. His work is for sale at Gallery Moderne, 1224 Washington Avenue, open Monday through Saturday from 10:00 a.m. to 5:00 p.m. and Thursday through Saturday evenings from 6:00 to 10:00 p.m. The downstairs exhibition shows works by other local artists. To get into the spirit of Deco dressing (or find vintage clothing from other eras), check out Last Tango in Paradise, 1214 Washington Avenue, open Monday through Thursday from 2:30 to 10:30 p.m., Friday and Saturday from 2:30 p.m. to 12:00 midnight. Decolectable, at 233 Fourteenth Street, features antique housewares and is open Tuesday through Saturday from 11:00 a.m. to 7:00 p.m. Virginia, the owner of Rubye's at 428 Espanola Way, is one of the area's more personable shop owners, and the clothing she sells is reasonably priced. Her store is open Monday through Thursday from 4:00 to 8:00 p.m., Fridays from 12:00 noon to 8:00 p.m., and Saturdays from 12:00 noon to 6:00 p.m. Even less expensive is My Uncle at 1570 Washington Avenue, open Monday through Saturday from 11:00 a.m. to 8:00 p.m.

Sip a tiny cup of sweet, sticky Cuban coffee, as the locals do, at any Cuban cafeteria or *bodega* (Cuban grocery) along Washington Avenue. You'll find some of the best ice cream in south Florida at The Frieze, 117 Fifth Street (almost to Ocean Drive).

▲▲ **South Point**—Below the Deco District, what was once Miami Beach's worst slum is fast becoming one of its more desired locations. At the very tip of Miami Beach is a park with barbecue grills, picnic tables, exercise equipment, walking paths, lookout towers, and a long fishing pier. They frequently bring bands to the amphitheater for neighborhood parties on weekends. From South Point, you get a great view of the Miami skyline. Try it at sunset.

▲▲ **Lincoln Road**—During the 1940s and 1950s, this was the posh "Fifth Avenue of Miami Beach." Later, the wealthy moved farther north; South American economies were going strong, though, and the shops turned to discount electronics and clothing, catering mainly to Venezuelans and Argentines who came to Miami Beach on major shopping sprees and returned to their countries loaded down with extraordinary amounts of "American" goods (mostly made in Asia), which they would sell at a profit. The Venezuelan oil boom busted, Argentina's peso plummeted, these shops became obsolete, and Lincoln Road became a vacant street offering cheap rents to anybody who wanted these foreken storefronts. That's when the artists moved in.

Now for pedestrians only, much of Lincoln Road remains empty, but renovation work is being done, especially between Meridian Avenue and Lenox. Books and Books, the largest non-chain bookstore in the Miami area, has its second store at 933 Lincoln Road. The South Florida Art Center at 901 Lincoln Road is a conglomeration of small studios under one roof where you can see the artists at work. A local artists' hangout is the Wet Paint Café, 915 Lincoln Road, next to the art center and the Miami City Ballet's rehearsal studios, where you can watch through the large window opening onto Lincoln Road as Miami's premier ballet company practices. Among the many fine art galleries on Lincoln Road, our favorite is the Skolsky Gallery, 1035 Lincoln, open Wednesday through Sunday from 12:00 noon to 6:00 p.m.

When you reach the end, you can breeze back down Lincoln
Road on a free tram with pink buildings painted all over it.
▲ **Bass Museum of Art**—The smaller Deco sector north of
Lincoln Road to 24th Street is called the Museum District
because the Bass Museum is in the middle of it. Though small,
the museum has good selections of contemporary and classical
art as well as temporary exhibits of local interest such as Latin
American artists and Miami area architecture. It is located at 2121
Park Avenue, open Tuesday through Saturday from 10:00 a.m. to
5:00 p.m. and Sunday from 1:00 to 5:00 p.m. Admission is $2 for
adults, $1 for students, and free for children under 17; free for
everybody on Tuesdays.

Check out the oceanfront boardwalk that stretches from 21st
Street to 46th Street.

Food

In 1913, when Miami Beach was still a little fishing village, a restaurant called **Joe's** opened up. Since then, it has grown into a
quality restaurant with award-winning food and a take-away
section on one side. Joe's specializes in local stone crabs, which
are served cold with hot melted butter and eaten with one's
fingers. Also on the menu are other seafoods, frog legs, steaks,
and traditional Floridian Key lime pie. Prices are moderate. Joe's
is located at the south end of Miami Beach at 227 Biscayne
Street (673-0365, take-away orders 673-4611). Lunch is served
Tuesday through Saturday from 11:30 a.m. to 2:00 p.m., and dinner is served daily from 5:00 to 10:00 p.m. Joe's is closed during
the summer months (June-September).

Puerto Sagua was an institution in pre-Castro Havana. After
the revolution, the owners took their name and fame to 700
Collins Avenue on Miami Beach. Everyone, of all ages, from the
local police to those they arrest, eats at Puerto Sagua. Film crews
and models share the counter with elderly ladies taking a break
from rolling their groceries home in little shopping carts. This is
the best place in town to eat Cuban food and view neighborhood life. The humorous 3-D paintings of life in Cuba that
decorate the walls were done by the locally famous Schull sisters, whose artwork you'll see more of around town. The food
at Puerto Sagua is plentiful and cheap. For breakfast, have *café
con leche* (espresso and milk) and Cuban toast, as the locals
traditionally do, or order one of their Spanish-style omelets if
you have a hearty appetite. For lunch and dinner, Puerto Sagua
specializes in seafood, but the daily specials of traditional
Cuban foods usually cost under $5 for more food than you can
eat. Hours are 7:30 a.m. to 2:00 a.m. daily.

For a casual but stylish meal, complete with ocean breeze, go
to the **News Café** at 800 Ocean Drive. The desserts are deli-

cious, but they sell out fast. You can also choose from an assortment of cold cuts, salads, breads, and granola, or opt for a more romantic combination—chocolate fondue for two served with champagne. The café also offers beer, wine, Pelligrini water, and various coffees. A good selection of books, magazines, and newspapers are for sale, and you're welcome to read at your table. Prices are moderate. Hours are from 9:00 a.m. to 1:00 a.m. daily, until 2:00 a.m. on weekend nights.

Another moderately priced restaurant is **The Strand** at 671 Washington Avenue. Reservations are suggested—call 532-2340. It is only open for dinner, daily from 6:00 p.m. to 2:00 a.m., until 3:00 a.m. on weekend nights. The menu changes every day but always includes homemade meatloaf and sandwiches as well as more expensive gourmet entrées. The bar is a popular social spot.

Crawdaddies, 1 Washington Avenue, is strategically located at the bottom of Miami Beach with a beautiful view of the Miami skyline and Biscayne Bay. You may see a cruise ship as it glides past. You can have drinks outdoors or eat inside the antique-laden restaurant from 11:00 a.m. to 11:00 p.m. daily. Prices are moderate.

Toni's, at 1208 Washington Avenue, features "New Tokyo Cuisine," a combination of Japanese and Continental cooking. They have reasonably priced sushi in a wide variety, which you can eat either at the traditional Japanese sushi bar or at a table. For dessert, try green tea ice cream or fried cheesecake. Lunch is served Tuesday through Friday from 12:00 noon to 2:30 p.m. and dinner from 5:30 to 10:30 p.m. nightly, until 11:30 on weekend nights.

Pineapples at 530 41st Street serves natural food and luscious desserts at moderate prices, open daily 10:00 a.m. to 10:00 p.m. For heavy-duty macrobiotic cuisine that tastes good, **The Place** at 830 Washington Avenue is the place, open Monday through Thursday from 11:00 a.m. to 8:00 p.m., Friday and Saturday from 11:00 a.m. to 11:00 p.m. They have a stage where live folk music is performed on weekends. Try a shot of wheatgrass juice tea for a pleasant aftertaste and healthy effects.

An old-time Miami Beach classic is **Wolfies** at 2038 Collins Avenue, serving Jewish deli fare 24 hours a day.

Casona de Carlitos brings the atmosphere of Buenos Aires' famous Boca neighborhood to Miami Beach. They have excellent steaks and chicken with rice. The clientele is truly South American, and they request their national songs from the singer and pianist who entertain Tuesday through Sunday. Located at 23rd and Collins, Casona de Carlitos is open daily from 12:00 noon to 12:00 midnight (more fun at night). Reservations are not needed, but there may be a short line at the door.

At the intersection of 13th and Ocean Drive are two Art Deco cafés, the **Cardozo** and the **Carlysle**, both beautifully decorated, both featuring live jazz. Ask about Marie, an endearing fortune-teller in her late 80s who will tell your fortune for a donation (at least $10 is the norm). Marie was given a key to the city of Miami Beach for her many years of friendship and advice from the porches of the Carlysle and Cardozo.

On the upscale side, there's **Lucky's**. You may recognize the interior from many episodes of *Miami Vice*. It is done up in 1930s Deco with splashy modern touches. Background piano music accompanies the excellent service. Delicious, exotic dishes fill your conversation with "What is it?" Try stuffed quail with couscous and other goodies on the side. For dessert, the specialties are soufflés made to order and chocolate "gifts" — chocolate meringue, fudge sauce, and raspberries, painstakingly wrapped in real chocolate paper with a chocolate bow. It's at 640 Ocean Drive. For reservations, call 538-1611. Dinner is served Monday through Thursday from 7:00 to 11:30 p.m., Friday and Saturday from 6:00 to 12:00 midnight, and Sundays from 6:00 to 10:00 p.m.

Scratch was converted into a restaurant, bar, theater, and dance club from an old Rolls-Royce repair garage. The menu changes daily but always lives up to the name, every tasty dish being made from scratch. Located at 427 Jefferson Avenue, it is open daily from 5:00 p.m. to 3:00 a.m., until 5:00 a.m. on weekend nights. Call 532-8315 for reservations. It's slightly expensive.

Café des Artes has a beautiful oceanfront garden setting and fine food. Prices are high, but the management is perfectionist about their food, atmosphere, and service. Located at 918 Ocean Drive, it is open Tuesday through Sunday from 6:00 to 11:00 p.m. Call 534-6267 for reservations.

Two elegant, very fashionable, and not cheap Italian restaurants are **Osterio del Teatro** at 1443 Washington Avenue, open daily from 6:00 to 11:00 p.m., until 12:00 midnight on weekend nights, reservations 538-7850, and **Mezzanotte**, which bathes its corner of 12th and Washington in hot pink lighting. Mezzanotte's windows face both streets, showing passersby how full the place is. For reservations, call 673-4343. Hours from 6:00 p.m. to 12:00 midnight daily, until 2:00 a.m. on weekend nights.

An unusual treat is kosher Chinese cuisine at the **Peking Embassy**, 1417 Washington Avenue. They have been in business since the 1940s, and although the decor is plain, the food has remained consistently good over the years. It's a little high-priced. Hours are Sunday through Thursday, 4:00 p.m. to 9:00 p.m. Call 538-7550 for reservations.

The **Fairmont** is a refreshing outdoor garden restaurant that resembles a cruise ship deck during the day and a romantic hideaway at night. Sunday brunch is excellent. It includes all the champagne you want and Caribbean music. Prices are around $15 per person. The Fairmont is located on the corner of 10th Street and Collins Avenue.

Hungry at odd hours? Have a late night snack at the **Sand-wicherie**, 229 14th Street, open daily from 10:00 a.m. to 6:00 a.m. It is a standup window with good sandwiches and always some tastefully unusual imported music.

Finally, for some real bargains: the **Villa Deli** at 1608 Alton Road features huge 98-cent breakfasts from 6:00 a.m. to 10:00 a.m. **Granada**, a Cuban café across from the youth hostel, has complete breakfasts for 99 cents until noon.

Tempt yourself with cookies and pastries at the **La Guardia Bakery**, 1141 Washington Avenue, open daily from 6:00 a.m. to 7:00 p.m. The open fruit market on 13th Street and Washington Avenue has the best selection of fresh fruit and vegetables in town.

Nightlife

Old Miami Beach is where Miamians and hip folks from Fort Lauderdale come for a night out.

Club Nu is the major nightclub in town, located at 245 22nd Street, open Wednesday through Sunday. People don't start coming until after 10:00 p.m. The drink of preference is expensive Perrier Jouet champagne, served from handpainted bottles. Wednesday is ladies' night, so women don't pay the cover charge and receive free champagne (of a cheaper brand) all night long. Every few months, Club Nu changes its decor — ancient Egyptian, Oriental, or Renaissance. Entertainment is an assortment of live acts, fashion shows, and the well-known Club Nu Dancers, who pose in sexy clothing that matches the club's current theme. The cover charge varies according to the entertainment. For current information, call 672-0068.

Deco's is a popular dance club for the younger set. It was converted from a fancy theater. At 1235 Washington Avenue, it is open Wednesday through Saturday from 8:30 p.m. to 5:00 a.m. The cover charge depends on the program.

Penrod's is a mega-conglomeration of ten bars, three restaurants, a pool, and a shop along the beach at 1 Ocean Drive. Hours are 11:00 a.m. to 5:00 a.m. On weekends, the crowd is mostly noisy college students, but the rest of the week anybody goes.

The back room at **Scratch** (see the Food listings above) sometimes becomes a theater. For more information, call 663-0208.

Then, on Thursday through Saturday nights from 11:00 p.m. on, it becomes a dance club. There is a $5 cover charge on weekend nights, but not on Thursdays.

For glow-in-the-dark decor, unpretentious attitudes, and lots of dancing, go to the **Kitchen Club** at 100 21st Street, open Tuesday through Sunday from 10:00 p.m. to 5:00 a.m.

Opened in 1926, **Club Deuce** is an ever-popular bar that sells pizza by the slice and has a compact disc jukebox and a pool table. Take a look at their vintage menu, from back when lobster cost 85 cents. *Miami Vice* and several movies have been filmed there. At 222 14th Street, it's open daily from 7:00 a.m. to 5:00 a.m.

A Caribbean-style bar called the **Island Club**, on the corner of Seventh Street and Washington Avenue, features an art gallery inside, as well as a compact disc jukebox and Ping-Pong tables. Caribbean food is served, and the clientele is a casual local crowd. Hours are 5:00 p.m. to 5:00 a.m. daily.

Along Ocean Drive, you can dip in and out of several open-air clubs, including **Waves**, 1060 Ocean Drive, which has music seven nights a week and no cover charge. **The Tropics**, 960 Ocean Drive, has late shows. Cover depends on the show. Check out the swimming pool with a mural on the bottom. A popular meeting place featuring 1950s architecture and more of that pink neon is the **Clevelander** at 1020 Ocean Drive.

Want to try some old-fashioned ballroom dancing on the cheap? Head to the **Oceanfront Auditorium**, 1001 Ocean Drive, on Sunday or Wednesday. From 8:00 to 10:00 p.m., you can dance the night away with the local senior citizens (who are known to get quite lively to the live vintage dance music). The entrance fee is $1.

Aside from nightclubs, consider a few other Miami Beach nightlife possibilities. You might take a horse and buggy ride through Old Miami Beach for $5 per person (two-person minimum), leaving from Ocean Drive. Major live theaters include the **Jackie Gleason Theater of the Performing Arts** (known as TOPA), located at 1700 Washington Avenue. It hosts major concerts, Broadway productions, and ballet. For information on current programs, call 673-8300. The **Cameo Theater** at 1445 Washington Avenue features rock and reggae concerts; call 532-0922.

Away from the beach, the city of Miami offers many more intriguing nightlife possibilities. Here are our favorites. Miami's oldest club is **Tobacco Road**, which features live blues bands nightly, two bands on weekends. Located at 626 Miami Avenue in a funky maritime neighborhood, Tobacco Road opens at 11:00 a.m. and has a cover charge of $5 on weekends. Steaks,

burgers, and seafood are served. Closing time is 5:00 a.m.
Flamenco music and dancing in an authentic Spanish-style setting can be found at **Málaga**, 740 S.W. Eighth Street, from 9:00
p.m. to 1:00 a.m. There is a two-drink minimum. For an exotic
night of Haitian music and dancing in the heart of Little Haiti,
go to **Obsession**, 69 N.E. 79th Street. They feature live bands
on Fridays and Saturdays, fashion shows, and Haitian food. The
cover charge varies.

Helpful Hints

For current information on local nightlife, restaurants, and the
arts, pick up a free copy of *New Times* on the street or in many
restaurants. Bulletin boards are at the International Youth Hostel
(1438 Washington Avenue) and The Place (830 Washington
Avenue).

The biggest annual event in Miami Beach is the Art Deco Fes-
tival, which fills Ocean Drive with music, dancing, food, and
antiques for sale. It happens in January. For specifics, contact
the Miami Design Preservation League at (305) 672-2014.

MIAMI

Miami is a new city, founded less than a century ago, but much has happened in that short time. While welcoming newcomers who pour in from snowy northern states, it has also assimilated waves of refugees from Europe, Cuba, Haiti, and Nicaragua. In multicultural Miami, you can make the rounds of Latin America and much of the Caribbean within an area of a few miles. The city's laid-back, tropical exterior conceals a heart that beats a mile a minute.

Suggested Schedule

10:00 a.m.	Go shopping in downtown Miami. Ride the Metromover.
12:00 noon	Lunch and shopping at Bayside.
2:00 p.m.	Visit Key Biscayne.
8:00 p.m.	Dinner in Little Havana.
10:00 p.m.	Stroll in Coconut Grove. Perhaps hit some nightspots there.
3:00 a.m.	Snacks at La Carretta or Versailles.

Miami

At ground level, downtown Miami resembles a small Latin American city. You can buy tropical fruit on the street and bargain for merchandise in small shops. Look up, and the future is abuzz overhead, with the Metrorail headed one way, the Metromover headed the other, and a skyline of daringly modern architecture that would outrage residents of more conservative American cities. It makes Miamians smile. The Centrust Building lights up on holidays in different colors. The Metrorail tracks sport multicolored fluorescent neon. Farther down, on Brickell Avenue, buildings are constructed with holes in the middle or painted with every color you'd find in a big box of crayons.

Miami is a city of "now you see it, now you don't." Last year's supermarket may now be the site of a Spanish-speaking shopping mall. The service station where you buy gas today may be a charismatic church tomorrow. Everything changes constantly. Until recently, the bayfront area across the street from downtown was only frequented by deviants and pickpockets. Now it is Bayside, a shopping, eating, and entertainment complex where people enjoy themselves without fear day and night.

What was once a rundown section of town became bustling Little Havana, and the area is now turning Nicaraguan as Cubans move out to suburbia and new waves of refugees move in.

Suburban areas that Miami has engulfed include Coconut Grove, a predominantly wealthy area where homes are secluded by lush foliage. The business district is packed with ritzy restaurants and boutiques—not a place to do practical shopping, but people spend hours strolling the streets and window-shopping. Coconut Grove is synonymous with money, and jet-setters and foreign royalty go there to play.

Another surrounded suburb, Coral Gables has remained its own city. Developed by George Merrick in the 1920s, it is a study in moneyed elegance. All of the homes are tastefully coordinated in pastel colors (a city ordinance prohibits garishness). Much of the architecture is Spanish style, and the streets have Spanish names—given to them by Merrick long before Latin American culture became a major Miami influence.

Finding Your Way Around

Miami is divided into quadrants: Northeast, Northwest, Southeast, and Southwest. The dividing streets are Flagler and Miami Avenue, so everything north of Flagler and east of Miami Avenue is a Northeast address; Southwest means south of Flagler and west of Miami Avenue. Be careful not to confuse streets, avenues, terraces, and courts, which may have the same number but be miles away from one another. Streets run east and west, avenues north and south. Terraces run parallel to streets of the same number, while courts parallel avenues. Just southwest of downtown lies a small, extremely confusing pocket of diagonals called roads. If you find yourself in this maze, look on the map and find your way out quickly.

Coral Gables streets have names instead of numbers, and so do those in Coconut Grove. If you accidentally find yourself in a suburb called Hialeah, in the northwest part of greater Miami, streets change to East and West designations.

Dixie Highway is a major north-south diagonal thoroughfare. In the north it is West Dixie, East Dixie, and Biscayne Boulevard, which reaches all the way downtown, then becomes Brickell Avenue, then South Dixie Highway. All of this is US 1.

Interstate 95 is the most important north-south freeway, and the easternmost. Farther to the west is Highway 826, or "The Palmetto," also a north-south freeway. Both of them end up on South Dixie Highway. The westernmost north-south freeway is Florida's Turnpike. All of these freeways converge at N.W. 167th Street in what is known as "The Cloverleaf," a mish-mash of ramps and signs that you should watch carefully.

Highway 836 is the main east-west freeway. It goes from
Miami Beach on the east to Florida's Turnpike on the west. A
shorter east-west freeway called 195 goes from Miami Beach to
the airport.

Public Transportation
The Metro Bus is efficient in both downtown Miami and Miami
Beach but lethargic in other areas. For schedule information,
call 638-6700. The fare are $1. Transfers, which cost $.25, can
also be used on Metrorail. Metrorail is Miami's elevated equiva-
lent to a subway. It is clean, modern, and rarely crowded. It
offers overhead views of several residential neighborhoods and
ghettos but does not reach many tourist destinations; it also
does not go to Miami Beach. The Metromover, a miniature version of the Metrorail, serves downtown Miami only (see the
Sightseeing Highlight below).

Sightseeing Highlights
▲▲ **Downtown Miami**—Walk and take in the atmosphere.
Many small shops sell clothing, shoes, and fabrics at discount
prices. Cuban cafeterias abound, along with one of Miami's
newer phenomena—Brazilian restaurants and shops catering to
newly arrived Brazilian clientele. Gusman Hall, at 174 East
Flagler Street, is an old-time theater that has preserved its vintage decor and has starlike lights on the ceiling. Many concerts
are performed here; for current information, stop at the information booth outside the theater or call 358-3338.
▲▲ **Bayside**—This complex of shops, restaurants, and entertainment at 401 Biscayne Boulevard has an excellent view of the
bay and marina. Shops include several small kiosks with African, Brazilian, Indonesian, and American Indian handicrafts.
Café Breselien has an authentic Brazilian samba band and
dancers at night. Bayside also houses Japanese, Spanish, and
Cuban restaurants and has an upstairs section of fast-food
stands specializing in everything from Middle Eastern food to
fudge and brownies. On weekends, live bands play day and
night at Bayside, and street performers entertain locals and out-
of-town visitors alike.
▲▲ **The Metromover**—For just 25 cents, you can ride the
Metromover from Bayside to any of its frequent stops. Here are
the best: Miami Dade Community College, 300 N.E. 2nd Avenue, often has outdoor activities and free noontime shows. (For
information, call Lively Arts, 347-3010). Also check out the
Inter-American Art Gallery on campus. The Metro-Dade Cultural Center, a new Mediterranean-style complex at 101 West
Flagler, contains two museums and Miami's main library. The
Museum of South Florida (375-1492) focuses on the history of

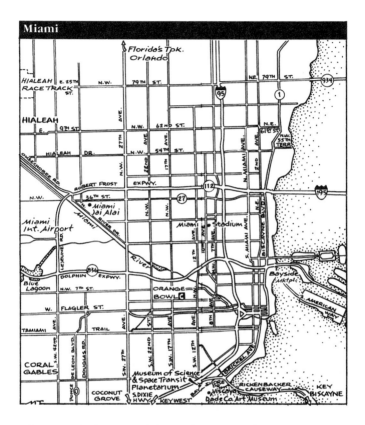

Miami, south Florida, and the Caribbean, and has some Native American exhibits. Hours are Monday through Saturday 10:00 a.m. to 5:00 p.m., until 9:00 p.m. on Thursday evenings, and Sundays from 12:00 noon to 5:00 p.m. Admission is $3 for adults, $2 for children ages 6 to 12. The Center for Fine Arts (375-1700) houses exhibits of internationally renowned artists. Hours and admission fees are the same as at the Museum of South Florida, except that the art museum is closed on Mondays. Combination tickets for admission to both museums are available for $5 per adult, $3 for children ages 6 to 12. The Miami-Dade Library (375-2665, also has a small art museum.

▲▲ **Key Biscayne**—South of downtown is the Rickenbacker Causeway ($1 toll), which has several beaches. Follow the turn-off signs to newly renovated Virginia Beach, Crandon Park, or Bill Baggs State Park, the most natural of the beaches, which has an entrance fee of $1 per vehicle and 50 cents per person. It is located at the very end of Key Biscayne and has a lighthouse

restored to its original 1830s condition. Wild raccoons scavenge
for your picnic leftovers; don't get too close—they bite.

Tourist attractions along the Rickenbacker Causeway include
the **Miami Marine Stadium** (3601 Rickenbacker Causeway,
361-6732), which hosts regattas, hydroplane races, and the
annual Pops by the Bay summer concert series. The **Seaquar-
ium** at 440 Rickenbacker Causeway (361-5703) is home to Flipper, the dolphin of TV fame, and a whale named Lolita. They
also have diving shows and one of the first manatees born in
captivity, along with tropical aquariums and exhibits. Hours are
9:30 a.m. to 6:30 p.m. daily. Admission is $13.95 for adults and
$9.95 for children age 12 and under. Allow three-and-a-half
hours to see all the shows. Across the street at 3979 Rickenbacker Causeway is **Planet Ocean** (361-9455), a marine science
museum with "hands-on" exhibits. You can touch an iceberg,
feel the force of a hurricane, and walk through a giant drop of
ocean water to see the life within. Hours are 7:00 a.m. to 4:30
p.m. daily. Admission is $7.50 for adults, $4 for children ages 6
to 12.

Back on land, just south of the Rickenbacker Causeway is
Vizcaya Museum and Gardens, 3251 South Miami Avenue,
579-2813 or 579-4626. Built in 1916 as the winter home of
industrialist James Deering, it is a fabulous 34-room Italian
Renaissance palace on ten acres of landscaped gardens overlooking Biscayne Bay. Antique furnishings and decor represent
Renaissance, baroque, rococo, and neoclassical styles. Trails
lead through a natural forest hammock. Hours are 9:30 a.m. to
5:00 p.m. daily. Admission is $6 for adults, $4 for senior citizens,
students, and children ages 6 to 12.

Across the street from Vizcaya at 3280 South Miami Avenue is
the **Miami Museum of Science/Planetarium** (museum—
854-4247; planetarium—854-2222). Coral reef exhibits, space
exhibits, and laser light shows make this a fun place, especially if
you are traveling with children. Planetarium director Jack Hork-
heimer is known to astronomy buffs as public TV's late-night
"Star Hustler." Hours are 10:00 a.m. to 6:00 p.m. daily. Admission to the museum is $4 for adults and $2.50 for senior citizens
and children ages 3 to 12; to the planetarium, $5 for adults and
$2.50 for seniors and children; or to both the museum and the
planetarium, $7 for adults and $4 for seniors and children.

▲▲**Coconut Grove**—South Miami Avenue soon becomes
Bayshore Drive and leads you past extravagant mansions to
Coconut Grove. Ralph Munroe settled in Coconut Grove in
1891; his house, **The Barnacle**, is now a park and museum at
3485 Main Highway. Main Highway is also the major thoroughfare through Coconut Grove's business district, which is lined
with sidewalk cafés, specialty shops, and boutiques. The

Coconut Grove Playhouse features first-rate plays from October to June. For information, contact Coconut Grove Playhouse, 3500 Main Highway, 442-4000.

Miami's most ostentatious shopping center, fun for window-shopping day or night, is the **Mayfair** at 2911 Grand Avenue. It is decorated with fountains, broken tiles, and cement relief—tiny details everywhere you look. The shops contain pricey clothing and artwork. The Mayfair also has several ritzy clubs.

Main Highway and Grand Avenue join at Five Corners, where several other streets also converge. Head east and you reach Biscayne Bay. Go west on Grand and you'll soon find yourself in a humble black neighborhood with colorfully painted stores and wooden signs handpainted by local artists. This area dates back before the turn of the century, when Bahamian immigrants settled in the Grove. You can still see early wooden homes along Charles Avenue.

▲▲**Coral Gables**—Northwest of Coconut Grove, this area was an early example of a planned community. Everything was done in Spanish style, including elaborate entrances, fountains, and plazas. Most of the streets are named after places in Spain. You can get a self-guided tour map locating over 100 sights at the Coral Gables Chamber of Commerce, 50 Aragon Avenue. The **Coral Gables House** at 907 Coral Way, now a museum, was the boyhood home of George Merrick, who developed Coral Gables. The **Venetian Pool** at Almeria Avenue and Toledo Street was a stone quarry from which building material for the city was taken. It is now a beautiful public swimming pool with tropical foliage, palm trees, islands, caves, and arched bridges. For hours and admission charges, call 442-6483.

Art lovers must see the University of Miami's **Lowe Art Museum**, on campus at 1301 Stanford Drive. Exhibitions of international artwork change frequently but are always outstanding. For current information, call 284-3535. Hours are Tuesday through Friday and Sundays from 12:00 noon to 5:00 p.m., Saturdays from 10:00 a.m. to 5:00 p.m., closed Mondays. Admission fees are $2 for adults, $1 for senior citizens and students, free for children under age 16. Another important art museum is the **Metropolitan Museum of Art Center** at 1212 Anastasia Avenue. It has a small but excellent permanent collection of Chinese and pre-Columbian art.

Main street Coral Gables is called **Miracle Mile**—slightly less than a mile of tasteful boutiques leading to Coral Gables City Hall. During the Christmas season, Miracle Mile and the city hall are resplendent with lights, decorations, and an elaborate Nativity scene with Santa's house on one side. Coral Way and Alhambra Circle are lovely streets to drive down and look at homes. Coral Gables is known for its fine restaurants.

▲▲**Little Havana**—The main street is Eighth Street, better known as **Calle Ocho**. It is lined with restaurants, clubs, and cafeterias. One of the first neighborhoods settled by Cuban refugees around 1960, Little Havana was a rundown part of town at the time. Now it's sparkling and full of life. See if **Domino Park**, at Calle Ocho and 14th Avenue, is open. Older Cuban men have traditionally gathered here in the evening to play dominoes and discuss politics. The **Cuban Museum of Arts and Culture** at 1300 S.W. 12th Avenue, dedicated to the preservation of Cuba's prerevolutionary cultural heritage, features exhibits and events with Latin themes. Hours are 10:00 a.m. to 5:00 p.m. on weekdays and 1:00 p.m. to 5:00 p.m. on weekends. Donations are accepted.

▲**Little Haiti**—Since 1980, Haitians have been settling in large numbers in this area of Northeast Miami. From N.E. 46th Street to 79th Street, between North Miami Avenue and N.E. Second Avenue, you can see little shops, churches, restaurants, and clubs catering to Haitian people, selling Haitian-style goods, serving Haitian foods, and doing business in the Creole-French language of Haiti. A two-block area of N.E. 54th Street, from N.E. Second Avenue to North Miami Avenue, is lined with brightly painted shops.

▲**Opa Locka**—In the 1920s, pioneer aviator Glen Curtiss developed several communities in the Miami area, each with its own architectural style. Opa Locka, built on an Arabian Nights theme, is impoverished and off the beaten track but of interest to architecture buffs. Though most of the buildings have deteriorated, the exotic city hall has been restored to its early splendor, as have a few other downtown structures. The main streets are laid out in the shape of a crescent moon and have Arabic names. Check out Shaherazad Street. To find Opa Locka, take Interstate 95 north to 135th Street and then head west.

Gambling (and Flamingos)—The flamingo, one of Florida's most familiar symbols, is not native to Florida. Stray flamingos that wander up from the West Indies are occasionally spotted in the wild, but most visitors to Florida will never see one. The best place we've found outside of zoos and animal parks to see real, live flamingos is at **Hialeah Racetrack** (horse racing), where a flamingo flock runs back and forth in the center area of the track. The racing season varies; for a current schedule, call 885-8000.

Pari-mutuel betting can also be found at the **Flagler Greyhound Track**, 401 N.W. 38th Court, 649-3000, where dog racing is held from April through June and from September through late October. You can bet on human competitors at the **Miami Jai Alai Fronton**, 3500 N.W. 37th Avenue, 633-9611.

This unusual sport from the Basque region of Spain is played year-round except October.

Flamingos can also be found on the lake at the **Parrot Jungle**, where trained parrots and macaws jump rope, roller-skate, and ride tiny bicycles. Located at 11000 S.W. 57th Avenue, it's open daily from 9:30 a.m. to 5:00 p.m. Admission is $9.75 for adults, $4 for children ages 3 to 12.

Food

Established in 1952, **Shorty's BBQ** continues to be a popular place to eat old-fashioned ribs for a reasonable price. You sit at a long wooden picnic table in this screened-in, non-air-conditioned, log cabin-style eatery at 9200 South Dixie Highway, 665-5732, open 11:00 a.m. to 10:00 p.m. daily.

El Cid looks like a Spanish castle. They have excellent Spanish and Continental dishes that are not cheap. Game meats are cooked before your eyes in an antique brick oven. It's located at 117 N.W. 42nd Avenue, open 12:00 noon to 1:00 a.m. daily. For reservations, call 642-3144.

Bayside's upstairs section has food booths from all over the world, and you can eat indoors or out with a view of Biscayne Bay.

A moderately priced Peruvian restaurant, **Salmon Salmon**, specializes in seafood and other traditional dishes. At 2907 N.W. Seventh Street, 649-5924, it is open from 12:00 noon to 10:00 p.m. daily. Try the fluorescent yellow *inka kola*.

Bangkok Bangkok is a very popular Thai restaurant at 157 Giralda Avenue in Coral Gables. Call 444-2397 for reservations.

Camis Seashells Restaurant at 6272 South Dixie Highway bathes you in soft pink neon light while you eat delicious, reasonably priced seafood. Call 665-1288 for reservations. Hours are daily from 5:00 p.m. to 10:00 p.m., weekend evenings until 11:00 p.m.

The **Argentine Mundial 78 Restaurant,** 2901 S.W. Eighth Street, 541-7773, is a tiny nook where tango singers hang out on Thursday nights. They serve authentic Argentine grilled steaks with a special sauce called *chimichurri*, made from garlic and marinated herbs. The steaks are best accompanied by an Argentine or Chilean wine. Prices are quite moderate, and the help is courteous and will understand when you point to the English side of the menu even though they don't speak the language. Reservations are usually unnecessary. Hours are from 11:00 a.m. to 11:00 p.m. daily. They serve inexpensive lunch specials Monday through Friday. Next door to Mundial 78 is an Argentine grocery that sells South American wines, *yerba mate* (a high-energy South American tea), *dulce de leche* (a caramel spread), and cassette tapes of tango music.

Zuper Pollo at 1247 Coral Way doesn't look like much from the outside, but inside, Argentine and Uruguayan specialties are served in an Uruguayan ranch atmosphere. Try *chivito al plato* (beef topped with bacon, ham, and melted cheese) or their homemade *gnoqu* pasta. Hours are Tuesday through Saturday from 12:00 noon to 11:00 p.m. (until 2:00 a.m. on weekend nights) and Sundays from 2:00 p.m. to 11:00 p.m.

Don't muddle through the maze of overpriced restaurants in Coconut Grove. For good food at moderate prices, go directly to the **Village Inn** restaurant and sidewalk café at 3131 Commodore Plaza, 445-8721, open daily from 11:00 a.m. to 2:30 a.m. **Mandarin Garden**, another good choice in Coconut Grove, has Mandarin and Szechuan food, a simple atmosphere, and very fast service. It's at 3268 Grand Avenue, 446-9999, open Monday through Thursday from 12:00 noon to 10:30 p.m., Friday from 12:00 noon to 11:30 p.m., and Saturday and Sunday from 4:00 p.m. to 11:30 p.m.

For a big splurge, the place is the **Two Sisters** restaurant in the Coral Gables Hyatt Hotel, 50 Alhambra Plaza, 441-1912. They serve excellent American and Continental cuisine to the accompaniment of strolling Paraguayan folk musicians from 7:00 to 11:00 p.m. nightly. Make reservations. They also serve breakfast (7:00-11:00 a.m.) and lunch (11:00 a.m.-2:30 p.m.).

Another splurge possibility, the **Crepe St. Michel** at 2135 Ponce de Leon Boulevard in Coral Gables, 446-6572, serves French food in a lovely atmosphere—piano, soft lights, and antiques. The murals on the walls are made from broken mirrors. Reservations are necessary. Lunch is served daily from 11:00 a.m. to 2:30 p.m., dinner from 6:00 p.m. to 11:00 p.m. (until midnight on weekend nights).

For a *little* splurge, one that may dent your pocketbook but not as seriously, eat at **Reflections**, an octagonal glass-enclosed restaurant overlooking Biscayne Bay. The food is good, and the atmosphere is just right. It's directly behind Bayside at 401 Biscayne Boulevard, 371-6433. Lunch is served Monday through Friday, 12:00 noon to 3:00 p.m., dinner daily from 6:00 p.m. to 11:00 p.m., Sunday brunch buffet from 12:00 noon to 3:30 p.m.

An inexpensive counter-style Cuban restaurant, where they quickly whip together a wide variety of giant sandwiches one after another before customers' eyes, is the **Latin American Cafeteria**, 2940 S.W. 22nd Street, open daily from 7:00 a.m. to 1:00 a.m.

Located in the heart of downtown at 127 S.E. First Street, **Gordo's** features Brazilian food. *Fejoada* (black beans and rice cooked with assorted cuts of pork) is Brazil's national dish. Food at Gordo's is cheap and plentiful. Hours are Monday through Saturday from 11:00 a.m. to 6:00 p.m.

A local Sunday tradition is to eat bagels and/or omelets at the **Brickell Emporium**, 1100 Brickell Plaza (a half-block west of Brickell Avenue), 377-3354. On Sundays, complimentary champagne is served. Inexpensive.

Versailles, 3555 S.W. Eighth Street, and **La Carretta**, 3652 S.W. Eighth Street, are casual, popular after-hours Cuban restaurants. They are famous for their extensive selections of desserts. In the wee hours on Friday and Saturday nights, incredibly dressed couples parade in from the extravagant Latin clubs nearby.

For great pork sandwiches, go to **La Lechaneria** at 3199 S.W. Eighth Street. Hours are daily from 9:00 a.m. to 1:00 a.m. (until 2:00 a.m. on weekend nights).

Ronald Reagan ate lunch at **La Esquina de Tejas**, and his table there has been roped off. Pictures of Reagan are everywhere in this restaurant, which also has good, cheap Cuban food. It is located at 101 S.W. 12th Avenue (also known as Ronald Reagan Avenue). It is open daily from 7:00 a.m. to 12:00 midnight.

The health food store in Unicorn Village, 16454 N.E. Sixth Avenue, 940-0187, sells natural foods, organic produce, and vitamins as well as natural cosmetics. They also have a gift shop specializing in crystals and occult books. The restaurant serves up healthy food, too. Hours are 8:00 a.m. to 10:00 p.m. daily.

Itinerary Option

A **Sea Escape** cruise to nowhere leaves Miami every Thursday at 10:00 a.m. and returns at 4:00 p.m., or you can take an evening cruise at 7:00 p.m., returning at 12:00 midnight. The cruises come complete with food, entertainment, and gambling for a modest $39 per person. Or $99 will get you on a Sea Escape cruise to Freeport in the Bahamas. For information and reservations, call (305) 379-0000, (800) 432-0900, or (800) 327-7400.

THE FLORIDA KEYS

Start your day underwater and discover the rare beauty of
Florida's living coral reef. Later, drive down to the southernmost point in the continental United States, arriving in Key West
for a traditional sunset celebration. En route, you won't have
time to visit all the sightseeing highlights we've listed. Don't
worry—save some. You'll be coming back this way in a couple
of days.

Suggested Schedule

9:00 a.m.	Drive to Key Largo.
10:00 a.m.	Snorkel at John Pennekamp Coral Reef State Park or tour the reef by glass-bottom boat.
12:00 noon	Drive down the Overseas Highway, visiting your choice of sightseeing highlights along the way.
5:00 p.m.	Arrive in Key West. Check into your accommo-dations for two nights.
Sunset	Sunset.
7:00 p.m.	Dinner.
Evening	Check out Ernest Hemingway's favorite bars.

Travel Route: Miami to the Florida Keys (161 miles)
From downtown Miami, find your way onto US 1 southbound
(the South Dixie Highway; either Brickell Avenue or I-95 will
take you directly there). Follow US 1 south all the way to Key
West, a distance of 161 miles. Once you pass the Home-
stead/Florida City area, it's virtually impossible to get lost.

Beginning at Key Largo, US 1 is known as the Overseas Highway. It is often busy, sometimes hazardous (watch out for trucks
in a hurry on this mostly two-lane route), but a unique motor-
ing adventure. On your left is the Atlantic Ocean, lined with
narrow, hard beaches of fossilized coral; the water is so shallow
that you can walk far out to sea without getting your bathing
suit wet. On your right is Florida Bay, a shallow expanse lined
with mangroves and studded with small, uninhabited islands;
the far shore of the bay is Everglades National Park. Mile mark-
ers (which are used as addresses in the Keys) descend from mile
107 on Key Largo to mile 0 at Key West.

Don't be dismayed by the many signs and billboards that
visually shout at you all along Key Largo. Many of the Florida
Keys are full of free enterprise, but you won't find high-rise

resort hotels and condos here because of the risk of hurricanes. Besides Key Largo (pop. 3,000), the other major towns on the way to Key West are Islamorada (pop. 1,500, with "suburbs" sprawling from mile 88 to mile 73) and Marathon (pop. 5,000, mile 53 to mile 47).

Just past Marathon, you'll cross Seven-Mile Bridge (miles 47 to 40), the longest in the Keys. Paralleling the modern bridge, you can see the original Seven-Mile Bridge that was part of Henry Flagler's Overseas Railroad from Miami to Key West until 1935, when a hurricane destroyed the rail route. You can still walk out on the old bridge, which is used for fishing, jogging, and roller skating.

You'll know you're getting close to Key West when you spot the big blimp tethered above Cudjoe Key at about mile 20. This is Fat Albert, owned by the Coast Guard. It carries sophisticated electronic surveillance equipment designed to spot smugglers. Smuggling drugs and/or refugees used to be a mainstay of Key West's economy back in the 1970s (but no longer, locals will assure you straight-faced).

Sightseeing Highlights
▲▲ Key Largo: John Pennekamp Coral Reef State Park—
Named for the Miami newspaper editor whose conservation efforts created both this underwater park and Everglades National Park, John Pennekamp State Park protects the best part of the only living coral reef in the continental United States and the 500 species of fish that inhabit it. To get there, watch for the road on the left not far past mile marker 103. Admission is $1.50 for the vehicle and driver and $1 for each passenger.

You can't see the reef from dry land; it's about five miles offshore. The glass-bottom boat *Discovery* leaves daily at 9:00 a.m., 12:00 noon, and 3:00 p.m. for 2½-hour tours of the reef. Be at the boat one hour before departure. Reservations are recommended, though often not necessary on the 9:00 a.m. tour. Fares are $10 for adults ($9 on the 9:00 a.m. trip), $5 for children ages 3 to 11. Call (305) 451-1621. The same phone number will give you current information on snorkel and scuba trips offered by the park's dive shop. Although the boat trip may sound simpler and drier, think again. Would you prefer to walk in the woods or watch them through a windshield? It's the same with the coral reef. Get in and play among the colorful dazzles of tropical fish. Watch weird sea creatures waving and wiggling below. Snorkeling, which is so easy that a complete novice can do it and emerge grinning, costs $18 per person for a trip of the same duration as the glass-bottom boat tour. A full day of scuba diving instruction on the reef costs about $70 per person. Seven other dive shops in Key Largo, all with big signs along the high-

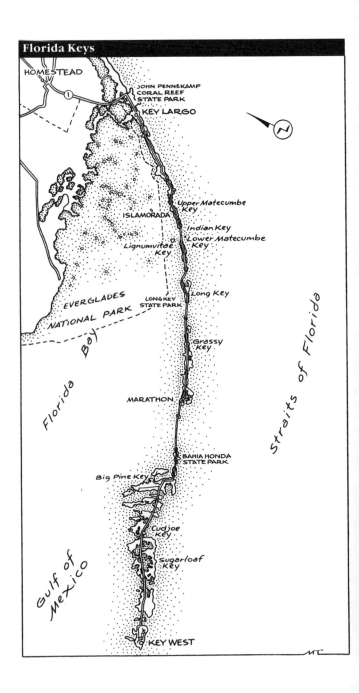

way, offer snorkel and scuba trips to John Pennekamp State Park and the adjoining Key Largo National Marine Sanctuary for about the same prices as in the park, so if the urge to snorkel strikes suddenly and you don't have reservations, don't worry—call around.

It is illegal to remove coral from any part of the reef, inside or outside the park. At one time, coral poachers used to loot it by the ton to sell for souvenirs, jeopardizing all life on the reef, but today all the coral you see in trinket shops comes from the Philippines, where the reefs are equally endangered but not protected.

▲▲ **Lignumvitae Key and Indian Key**—State-operated three-hour boat tours leave from the public boat launch at mile 79 on the Indian Key Fill between Upper and Lower Matecumbe Keys. The boat to Indian Key leaves at 8:30 a.m. and the one to Lignumvitae Key at 1:30 p.m., except Tuesdays and Wednesdays. The cost is $6 for adults and $3 for children under age 13. For information and reservations, write to Lignumvitae Key, P.O. Box 1052, Islamorada, FL 33036, or call (305) 664-4815.

Lignumvitae Key State Botanical Site, on the Florida Bay side of the fill, is said to be the last stand of virgin tropical forest in Florida, a solitary example of what most of the Upper Keys must have looked like when the first Europeans arrived. While the island's giant mahogany trees were cut 100 years ago and a single limestone house was built in 1919 where the boat now docks, the forest remains so close to primeval that the Nature Conservancy bought both Lingumvitae and Indian Keys in 1970 and made arrangements to turn them over to the state parks department. Besides the rare lignum vitae, the 133 species of tree that grow on this 345-acre island include such unusual ones as the mastic, poisonwood, pigeon plum, and gumbo limbo. One of the most bizarre is the strangler fig, which wraps around another tree of a different species until the two appear to be a single strange hybrid. In fact, the fig's seed only germinates when caught in the other tree's branches. Then it sends tiny filaments to earth which grow slowly into a trunk that wraps around the other tree's trunk and eventually, over many decades, chokes it to death.

On the Atlantic side of the fill, Indian Key State Historic Site is much smaller—about ten acres—and was completely developed in the 1830s, when it was the county seat of Dade County. Although the morning tour is hard to work into trip plans unless you spend a night in the Upper Keys, south Florida history buffs will find it interesting. Indian Key was the home of wrecker (some say outlaw) Jacob Houseman and tropical botanist Dr. Henry Perrine. In 1840, more than 100 Seminole Indians who had heard of the unscrupulous Houseman's plan to hunt them down and collect $200 "dead-or-alive" bounties, launched a preemptive strike in which nearly all structures on the island were destroyed and 16 residents were slain. Among the victims was Dr. Perrine. Houseman and his family escaped, never to return, and the ruins of Indian Key have been uninhabited for more than a century.

▲**Grassy Key: Dolphin Research Center**—Formerly a commercial attraction (Flipper's Sea School), the research center at mile 59 is a major facility for studying dolphin communications. It is also a vacation resort of sorts; dolphins from aquariums elsewhere in the nation are sometimes sent here to relax when they show stress symptoms. Tours of the facility are conducted Wednesday through Sunday at 9:30 a.m., 11:00 a.m., 1:00 p.m., and 3:30 p.m. Donations are accepted. For $40, you can spend 20 minutes swimming with the dolphins. For information or swimming reservations, contact Dolphin Research Center, P.O. Box Dolphin, Marathon Shores, FL 30352, (305) 289-0002.

▲**Bahia Honda State Park**—For a relaxing break from the Overseas Highway, the beach here is the best in the Keys, one of the few with sand. There is also a nature trail that takes you through a coastal hammock where rare trees and flowers grow, their seeds carried here from the Caribbean by birds, wind, and water. Snorkeling and scuba equipment, as well as windsurfers, are available for rent. Admission is $1.50 per car and driver, plus $1 per passenger.

▲**Big Pine Key: National Key Deer Refuge**—The smallest deer in North America is also the largest endangered land mammal in the Florida Keys. (The others are the wood rat and the cotton mouse, whose habitats have scuttled many development plans.) Adult Key deer stand only 30 inches high and weigh about 70 pounds. As a result of poaching, there were less than 50 of them left 40 years ago, and their impending extinction started the conservationist movement that resulted in modern laws protecting endangered species. Today, still endangered, the Key deer population has increased to about 350. The best time to see the deer is at dawn or dusk, but you might spot one in the undergrowth at any time of day as you walk the nature trails through pines, palms, and a tropical hardwood hammock. Watch for alligators around the "blue hole," a former quarry now flooded to create a large freshwater pond. To reach the refuge, turn onto Road 940 (Key Deer Boulevard), at the stoplight near mile 31, and go two miles. The visitors center is open Monday through Friday from 8:00 a.m. to 5:00 p.m.; the refuge is open daily from dawn to dusk.

Food

If you plan to snorkel this morning, eat a light breakfast (or none at all) before you go. When you return from the reef, a good breakfast spot is **Tony's**, across the highway from the John Pennekamp Coral Reef State Park entrance. Better yet, locals swear by the breakfasts at **Harriet's** toward the other end of town near mile 95.

A good lunch spot near the dock for tours to Lignumvitae and Indian Keys is **Papa Joe's** at mile 80 which opens at 11:00 a.m. (closed Tuesdays) and serves fresh, reasonably priced fish and seafood.

For dinner in Key West, there are many possibilities—almost all expensive. The newest and, locals say, best in town is **Mira** in the Marquesa Hotel, 600 Fleming, 296-5595. The menu is a mix of imaginative American, Italian, and French dishes. The prices are outrageously high—expect to spend $75 per person. For about half that price, you can dine at **Louie's Backyard**, 700 Waddell Avenue (at the other end of Duvall), 294-1061. Louie's is a Key West landmark, and reservations can be hard to get. Call early. **La-Te-Da** (La Terraza de Marti), 1125 Duvall, 294-8435; is slightly more affordable, with its prix fixe dinner served from 7:00 p.m. to 10:00 p.m. for about $30 per person.

Surveying these and many other trendy restaurants around Key West, you may understandably wonder whether there's any place in town where you can eat for less than the price of a day at Walt Disney World. Believe it or not, there is! Search out any of these: **El Miramar** (914 Kennedy Drive), **La Cubanita** (601 Duval Street #3), or **El Cacique** (125 Duval Street), all of which serve excellent, reasonably priced Cuban food; or **La Bodega** (829 Simonton Street) for soup, sandwiches, and decor consisting of many caged birds. For low-priced take-out barbecue sandwiches, until 9:00 p.m. (7:00 p.m. on Sundays), drive out to the **Hercules Bar-B-Q** at 3332 North Roosevelt Boulevard.

The unique local food specialties of the Florida Keys which you'll find ample opportunity to try are conch, prepared in dozens of different ways mostly designed to hide the unfamiliar taste, and Key lime pie, which, unlike elsewhere, is actually made from Key limes, a spiny little yellow fruit that doesn't taste like the limes you're used to.

Lodging

The most interesting places to stay in Key West are the numerous bed and breakfast guest houses in town. Reservations are essential, some have three-day minimum stay requirements at busy times of year, many of them won't accept children or pets, and a few are for gay men (or, in one case, women) only. Write

or call ahead to **Key West Reservation Service**, P.O. Drawer
1689, Key West, FL 33040; for information, call (305) 294-7713
or (305) 294-8850, or, to make reservations, (800) 356-3567
from Florida or (800) 327-4831 nationwide. Rates range from
$55 to $195 in season (December 15 to April 30), as low as $30
at other times of year. **Authors of Key West**, well located on
White Street in Old Key West, has nine cottages and rooms, each
named for an author who lived in Key West. Other nicely
restored Victorian era B&Bs include **Colours Key West** on
Fleming Street, **Key West Bed & Breakfast** on William Street,
Eaton Lodge on Eaton Street, and **La Terrazza de Marti** on
Duval Street. Key West Reservation Service also books resort
hotels, motels, vacation houses, condominiums, and
apartments.

Key West's best elegant small hotel is the new **Marquesa**, 600
Fleming Street, (305) 292-1919 or (800) 792-7637. It's somewhat
historic (it was a boarding house for a hundred years before its
recent face-lift) and has designer toiletries, a full-time con-
cierge, and maids who leave Godiva chocolates on the
pillows—all for $150 to $250 per night. Also upscale is **The
Reach**, 1435 Simonton at the ocean, (305) 296-5000 or (800)
874-4118, a long-established resort with the island's only private
natural beach. Rates are $200 to $425 per night. The Reach's
pier is one of the most romantic spots in Key West.

At the other end of the lodging spectrum, the **Key West Hostel** (AYH) at the **Sea Shell Motel**, 718 South Street, (305)
296-5719, offers dormitory beds at $11 a night for members, $14
for nonmembers, and budget motel rooms for under $40.

Camping

The only campground on Key West is **Jabour's Trailer Court**,
within walking distance of the old town at 223 Elizabeth Street,
(305) 294-5723. Sites with full hookups cost $23.

There is a KOA campground, **KOA Sugarloaf Key**, 20 miles
from Key West. It has a beach, a fishing bridge, and a marina
with boats and canoes for rent. Sites cost about $24. Aside from
being within driving distance of Key West, Sugarloaf Key is a
pretty unexciting place, but like most of the Keys, it has its oddi-
ties. Settled around 1900 by a British firm quaintly named the
Florida Sponge and Fruit Company, the island has as its major
landmark a 35-foot-tall bat tower, an early developer's
mosquito control scheme. (No bats ever moved in, though.) In
contrast to Key West's long list of local authors, Sugarloaf's only
famous sometimes-resident writer is Hunter S. Thompson. Ask
around for directions to the "nude canals."

The nearest state park campground to Key West is at **Bahia
Honda State Park**, 37 miles away, a short distance southwest

of Seven-Mile Bridge. (See the description in Sightseeing Highlights above.) Bahia Honda operates on a system whereby half the sites can be reserved ahead of time (call 305-872-2353 no more than 60 days in advance); the other half are first-come, first-served, but this isn't quite as simple as it sounds. "First-comers" start signing up in the morning, and the campsites are assigned at 3:00 p.m., so at busy times—most weekdays during the winter months—getting a site here without a reservation can be an all-day enterprise. Sites cost about $18.

Sunset

The traditional place in Key West to watch the sunset is **Mallory Square Dock**. Hippies picked this location in the late 1960s, gathering daily to watch through a marijuana haze as the sun swelled to many times its normal size, turned fantastic flamingo pink, and slid into the shimmering gulf. (Oh wow, far out!) The sunset is as psychedelic as ever, but these days you can barely glimpse it from Mallory Square. Instead, you'll see throngs of street performers and other strange local characters doing (and selling) strange local things—a perfect introduction to Key West.

If you'd prefer to meditate on the sunset itself, the best place to do it is **Fort Zachary Taylor State Historic Site** on the southwest tip of the island (take Southard Street), where you'll find Key West's best beach. The Civil War-era fort at the site has one of the largest collections of cannons anywhere and a historical museum. Admission is $.50 per vehicle and $1 per passenger (children under age six free). Park hours are from 8:00 a.m. to sunset; the fort area closes at 5:00 p.m.

Key West Nightlife

The first Key West nightspot that comes to anyone's mind is **Sloppy Joe's Bar**, 201 Duval Street (on the corner of Greene Street), 294-5717. Ernest Hemingway got drunk here. In fact, when Hemingway moved away from Key West, he stored boxes of personal effects, including unpublished manuscripts, in Sloppy Joe's back room, where they gathered mildew for 22 years until his death. Still "Hemingway's favorite bar," Sloppy Joe's is the place to see and be seen in Key West. It's open daily from 9:00 a.m. to 4:00 a.m., with live music every night. It's well worth a visit (if not the prices charged for the elaborate specialty drinks) to ponder what Hemingway would think if he could see the place now.

Equally historic is **Captain Tony's Saloon**, across the street from Sloppy Joe's at 428 Greene Street, 296-9417. The oldest bar in town, this was Hemingway's favorite for a while (it was the original site of Sloppy Joe's, which moved to the present location in 1937), but the memorabilia that decorate this place recount the exploits of the owner, Captain Tony Tarracino, locally notorious self-styled outlaw and former friend of Tennessee Williams. Tarracino was almost elected mayor of Key West in 1985. Hours are 12:00 noon to 4:00 a.m.

Nearby at 224 Duval Street are the **Bull** (downstairs, open at 10:00 a.m., Sundays at noon) and the **Whistle** (upstairs, open at 5:00 p.m., a great place to people-watch above Duval). Both bars close at 2:00 a.m. The Bull features loud live rock music nightly.

Barhopping is about all there is to do in Key West after dark. To quote the motto of **The Green Parrot**, another traditional hangout (Southard Street at Duval), "See the Keys on your hands and knees." From here, you're on your own. Tomorrow you don't have to go anywhere.

KEY WEST

Key West's past is long and checkered. Founded as a pirate hideout, the town has been home at various times to shipwreck salvagers, railroad builders, sponge divers, cigar rollers, smugglers, sailors, and eight Pulitzer Prize-winning writers. It has been the richest town per capita in the United States, and the poorest. Today, it is an artsy, conspicuously gay, self-consciously eccentric town of 25,000 where preservationists and developers battle over a severely limited supply of real estate. It is a fairly expensive resort destination, and children probably won't rate it among their favorite places in Florida, but go ahead and spend the extra few dollars. Don't just ride the Conch Train and then retreat to someplace cheaper. Give Key West a chance. Linger and bask in the giddy Conch version of "island consciousness."

Suggested Schedule

9:00 a.m.	Get oriented with a ride on the Conch Train.
10:30 a.m.	Tour Hemingway's house.
12:30 p.m.	Lunch.
1:30 p.m.	Visit the Wreckers' Museum or the Audubon House.
3:00 p.m.	Visit Mel Fisher's treasure museum.
Sunset	It happens every evening.

Key West
Key West is unlike the rest of the Florida Keys or, for that matter, anywhere else. Locals, known as Conchs (pronounced "Conks"), try hard to keep it that way and make it more and more different. The southernmost town in the continental United States, just a few miles from the Tropic of Cancer, Key West is closer to Havana, Cuba, than it is to Miami. Even more than in Miami, residents keep reminding you that this isn't mainstream America. Key West seceded from the Union and declared itself the Conch Republic on April 23, 1982, to protest border patrol roadblocks on US 1 where all vehicles coming from the Keys were searched for drugs and undocumented workers. The inspection stations were finally removed, and Civil War II thus averted, but Conchs never forget.

Key West is for walking. Unless you're staying in accommodations with a parking lot, leave your car at the Mallory Square parking lot ($1 for the first hour, $.50 an hour thereafter). For an orientation to the city, ride the Conch Train. This open-air tram pulled by a propane-powered jeep disguised as a locomotive covers 60 sights and sites along a 14-mile route—farther than you'd probably want to walk. The driver's nonstop narration is packed with odd historical tidbits and vintage gossip. The 1½-mile tour leaves frequently from Mallory Square and costs $8 for adults, $3 for children ages 3 to 11. The Old Town Trolley also offers narrated tours, following about the same route as the "train," and costs the same. It lets you get off where you wish and reboard a later trolley at no extra charge. It runs every half-hour and has 16 boarding stations around town including several hotels. If you just want to go somewhere, like from your lodgings to Mallory Square to catch the Conch Train, there are taxis. Some of them are pink—call 296-6666.

Sightseeing Highlights
▲▲▲**Ernest Hemingway Home and Museum**—This is the premier Key West attraction, the one folks back home will ask whether you saw. Ernest Hemingway lived in Key West from 1929 to 1940. At first he lived at 1100 South Street, where he finished *A Farewell to Arms*, but in 1931 he and his wife, Pauline, bought the mansion at 907 Whitehead which still bears his name. At the time, it was the grandest home in town. The wall around the house was built in 1937 from bricks that had once paved Duval Street, and Hemingway spent his last few Key West years reclusively behind it. In 1940, he and Pauline were divorced. She kept the house; he moved to Cuba.

In the upstairs study of the pool house out back, you can see the chair where Hemingway sat and the typewriter he used while writing *To Have or Have Not, Death in the Afternoon, The Green Hills of Africa,* "The Snows of Kilimanjaro," and *The Fifth Column.* Upstairs in the main house, sensitive visitors often report feeling the author's eerie presence. It's doubtful whether the resident ghost is really Ernest Hemingway's, since he died thousands of miles away, 21 years after he left Key West. When they moved into this house, Pauline Hemingway also complained that it was haunted. Anyway, somebody's ghost may be lurking here and occasionally giving tourists a chill. See if you feel it.

The Hemingway Home is open daily from 9:00 a.m. to 5:00 p.m. Admission is $3 for adults, $1 for children ages 4 to 12.
▲**Tennessee Williams House**—Key West's second-most famous writer lived for 34 years in the modest house at 1431 Duncan Street. It is a private residence, so you can only see the exterior. Preservationists hope to acquire it and turn it into a museum like the Hemingway Home in miniature. Williams never used Key West as the setting for any of his plays, but the

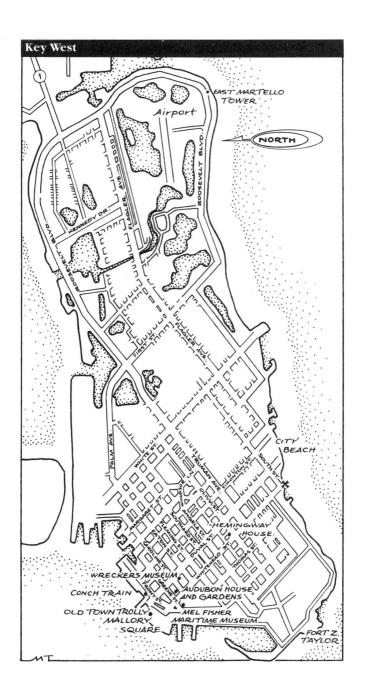

Key West

EAST MARTELLO TOWER

Airport

NORTH

ROOSEVELT BLVD.

KENNEDY DR.

FLAGLER AVE.

ROOSEVELT BLVD

FIRST ST.

FLAGLER AVE.

PALM AVE.

WHITE ST.

TRUMAN AVE.

SIMONTON ST.

SOUTH ST.

CITY BEACH

MARGARET ST.

OLIVIA ST.

DUVAL ST.

WHITEHEAD ST.

THOMAS ST.

HEMINGWAY HOUSE

FRONT ST.

GREENE ST.

WRECKERS MUSEUM

CONCH TRAIN

OLD TOWN TROLLY

MALLORY SQUARE

AUDUBON HOUSE AND GARDENS

MEL FISHER MARITIME MUSEUM

FORT Z. TAYLOR

MT

1956 motion picture version of *The Rose Tattoo*, starring Burt
Lancaster, was filmed at this house (while Williams was living in
it) and elsewhere in Key West.

Other authors who have lived in Key West include Elizabeth
Bishop, Truman Capote, James Leo Herlihy, John Hersey, Joseph
Lash, Alison Lurie, Carson McCullers, Thomas McGuane, James
Merrill, Gore Vidal, and Richard Wilbur.

▲▲**Audubon House and Gardens**—The first building in Key
West to be saved by preservationists, way back in 1958, this
historic home was never Audubon's. In fact, some local
historians say it hadn't been built yet when the ornithological
artist visited the Keys in 1832. Its only connection with
Audubon has to do with the decor, which includes several original engravings and a stuffed roseate spoonbill. (Despite popular
belief, Audubon was not a be-kind-to-the-birds kind of guy. He
shot them for sport as well as to use as models, and he per-
sonally killed hundreds in Florida Bay. In those days, endangered species were "preserved" in museums, and if they then
vanished from the wild, the collected specimens became more
valuable. In later years, Audubon complained that wildlife was
getting hard to find, and that observation inspired the National
Audubon Society, which has done more than any other conservation group to save endangered birds like the spoonbill.) There
is also a short film showing Audubon's paintings of south
Florida birds.

The Audubon House was built by Captain John Geiger, a Key
West wrecker during the early nineteenth century. Many of the
period antiques and furnishings were salvaged from shipwrecks
by Geiger and other Conchs. The Old Island Restoration Foun-
dation, responsible for most Key West historic preservation,
was originally formed to keep this house from being razed to
build a gas station. Located at the corner of Whitehead and
Greene streets, the house is open to the public daily from 9:30
a.m. to 5:00 p.m. Admission is $3 for adults, $1 for children ages
6 to 12.

▲▲**Wrecker's Museum (Oldest House)**—This former sea
captain's home at 322 Duval Street recalls the pre-Civil War era
when wrecking was the sole occupation in Key West. Before
lighthouses were built on the Florida Keys, the surrounding
waters were among the world's most treacherous. Local residents, most of whom had been marooned here themselves, salvaged the cargoes of hundreds of shipwrecks. To define the line
between wrecking (which was legal) and piracy (which was
not), wreckers were licensed and regulated, and a special court
was established in Key West to determine legal ownership of
goods from shipwrecks. Most of the antique furnishings in this
1829 house came from the holds of ill-fated ships. You can also

see model ships, a nineteenth-century dollhouse, and the original outdoor cookhouse. The museum is open daily from 10:00 a.m. to 4:00 p.m. Admission is $1.75 for adults, $.50 for children ages 3 to 12.

▲▲ **Mel Fisher's Maritime Heritage Society Museum**— While wrecking was big business in the Keys for only a few decades, ships have been sinking on the reefs for four centuries, from Spanish galleons to modern marijuana-smuggling boats such as the 65-foot vessel that lies off the Matacumbe Keys, its cargo intact but worthless. The biggest sunken treasure in Florida history was found by Mel Fisher in 1985. Fisher and his crew had spent fifteen years exploring and excavating the wrecks of two Spanish ships that sunk in 1622, the *Nuestra Señora de Atocha* and the *Santa Margarita*, which lie about 40 miles offshore, when they discovered a trove that included 47 tons of gold and silver and 70 pounds of emeralds. Today you can see—and even touch—examples from the *Atocha* treasure in Fisher's small museum at 200 Green Street, open daily from 10:00 a.m. to 6:00 p.m. Admission is $5 for adults, $4 for senior citizens, and $1 for children under 12—a small price to pay for the chance to hold an antique bar of pure gold.

▲ **Turtle Kraals**—Beside the Turtle Kraals restaurant at 101 Margaret Street, in what was once a slaughterhouse, is a small private museum where grisly photos and paraphernalia show all too graphically how green sea turtles came to the edge of extinction. The present owners have made the property into a breeding sanctuary for this endangered species. Turtle soup is still a favorite in several Key West restaurants, but today the main ingredient comes from commercial turtle farms around Lake Okeechobee. Admission is free.

▲ **East Martello Museum and Art Gallery**—Two "Martello towers"—fat, round bunkers shaped like Shriners' fezzes—were begun in 1862 to defend Key West's southern shore, but they were never completed. In 1950, the Key West Art and Historical Society took over the abandoned East Tower and made it into a museum where you can see works of art by illustrious locals as well as history exhibits ranging from the pirate era through the 1970 Mariel boatlift. A "writers' room" contains copies of practically all the books written in Key West. The tower is located on South Roosevelt Boulevard in front of the airport terminal. It is open daily from 9:30 a.m. to 5:30 p.m. Admission is $2.50 for adults, $.50 for children ages 7 to 15. (There is also a West Martello Tower, on Atlantic near the Monroe County Beach; it is the headquarters of the local garden club.)

▲ **Southernmost Point**—Follow Whitehead Street (which parallels Duval one block to the west) all the way to the intersection with South Street, and you can stand on the southernmost point in the continental United States.

FROM KEY WEST TO THE EVERGLADES

Drive back up the Keys and continue into Everglades National Park. When you finally arrive at Flamingo, the national park village on the north shore of Florida Bay, you'll be less than 30 miles due north of the Long Key Viaduct (mile 65 on the Overseas Highway). After the manic activity and all-night nightlife of Miami Beach and Key West, in Everglades National Park you'll experience something completely different: open spaces and silence.

Suggested Schedule

9:00 a.m.	Leave Key West. Drive the Overseas Highway again, stopping at sightseeing highlights you missed the first time.
2:30 p.m.	Arrive at the entrance to Everglades National Park.
4:00 p.m.	Arrive at Flamingo. Check into the lodge for two nights or find a campsite.
4:30 p.m.	If you want to take a sunrise canoe trip or boat cruise tomorrow morning, buy your tickets now at the marina.
Evening	Relax.

Travel Route: Key West to Homestead (128 miles) to Flamingo (46 miles)

Retrace your Day 10 route up the Keys and back to the mainland. At Florida City, on the southern outskirts of Homestead, turn left on Highway 27, following the big green signs to Everglades National Park.

The main park visitors center is on your right before you reach the entrance gate. If you're planning to camp, stop there first to check on campsite availability. If you have reservations at Flamingo Lodge, proceed directly there and check in.

Admission to the national park is $5 per vehicle. Keep your receipt, which will let you leave the park and reenter free for the next seven days. The driving distance from the park entrance to Flamingo is 38 miles; allow one to one-and-a-half hours nonstop for the drive. If you want to go on a sunrise canoe trip tomorrow, you must buy your tickets from the tour window at the Flamingo Marina store this afternoon before 5:00 p.m.

Food

The **Flamingo Restaurant**, the only one in the park, offers wonderful views of the bay and its birdlife along with an eclectic menu of Floridian and exotic dishes. The logical choice is seafood. Prices aren't cheap, but after Key West they look like bargains. Reservations are required for dinner. If you catch your own fish and clean it, the restaurant will gladly cook it, serve it, and charge you for it.

The Flamingo Marina store has a snack bar that serves sandwiches and soft drinks. It also carries a limited choice of grocery items for campers and picnickers, but you'd be wise to stock up at the supermarket in Florida City before entering the park.

Lodging

Again, the **Flamingo Lodge** has the only beds in the park. In season (November through April), a motel-style room with two double beds costs $69 a night, a cottage with a kitchen costs $80, and a suite costs $105. No pets are allowed in guest rooms. To stay here, you must make reservations far in advance and pre-pay for one night within 14 days after you make them. Contact Flamingo Lodge, P.O. Box 428, Flamingo, FL 33030, (813) 695-3101 or (305) 253-2241.

There's a slim chance that Flamingo Lodge will have an available room if you arrive without reservations; there's a better chance that they won't. It's a long drive back to Homestead, where you'll find a full range of fairly ordinary motel accommodations but no bargains.

Camping

Everglades National Park has two campgrounds, each charging $7 per night—one of the best camping bargains in Florida.

The more popular campground, the only place to stay if you want to take an early morning or sunset boat tour, is **Flamingo Campground**, at the end of the road about a mile past the marina. It is a very large campground carved out of the mangrove jungle, all lawn and no shade, and there are a few mosquitoes even in winter, which is *not* mosquito season (thank goodness!), but don't let any of this daunt you. Flamingo is as far from civilization, and as close to the true wilderness, as your car can take you in south Florida.

The other campground, not far from the entrance gate, is **Long Pine Key Campground**. Sites here are nestled among tall pine trees, and it's not far to Royal Palm Visitor Center, where a sunset walk on the Anhinga or Gumbo Limbo trails will show you wildlife galore. The drawback to camping at Long Pine Key is that it makes a sunrise canoe trip practically impossible.

Sites at both campgrounds are first-come, first-served. Here's how it works: first stop at the main visitors center outside the park entrance and check the board behind the rangers' counter to find out whether either or both campgrounds have vacant sites. (Flamingo normally fills up first.) Drive directly to the campground of your choice. The fee stations are only open in the morning. The ranger writes the numbers of sites that have been vacated as of the time he goes off duty on a chalkboard outside the station. You can take any of those sites and erase the number. You can also take any other site that appears empty, though if someone shows up with a receipt showing that they paid for the site earlier, you'll have to move elsewhere. It's all very informal. Pay your campsite fee the next morning by 10:00, and if you want to stay a second night, pay for that too. (Then, if anybody occupies your campsite, they will have to move.)

Nightlife
You bet. Wear insect repellent and disregard scary noises.

EVERGLADES NATIONAL PARK

Experience the everglades before they're gone.

Suggested Schedule

6:00 a.m.	Canoe on Florida Bay at sunrise.
8:00 a.m.	Breakfast at Flamingo Lodge.
9:00 a.m.	Drive back toward the park entrance, stopping along the way to walk each boardwalk. Please don't pet the alligators.
1:00 p.m.	Hot, huh? Return to Flamingo for a nap or spend the afternoon at nearby Biscayne National Park or the zoo.
Sunset	This is the best time for wildlife viewing.

The Florida Everglades
Less than half of Everglades National Park consists of true ever-glades, the grassy seasonal wetlands that once covered most of south Florida, and only one-fifth of the original everglades are within the national park. Settlers and developers saw no value whatsoever in the everglades. In the first half of the twentieth century, the solution to the everglades "problem" seemed easy. Drain them and turn them into irrigated farmland. Bull-doze away the mangroves, build Miami, and use the everglades drainage to supply the burgeoning population with fresh water. That's exactly what Floridians did from Homestead and West Miami all the way to the south shore of Lake Okeechobee. Half of the everglades died before 1947, when a few influential peo-ple stopped saying "So what?" and, realizing that south Florida had a genuinely unique, endangered ecosystem on its hands, won national park status for the most remote part of the ever-glades wilderness. The first road was not built through the park until 12 years later—in 1959.

Whether the everglades will survive remains an open ques-tion. The national park is now dependent on man for its fair share of irrigation from south Florida's complex, computer-controlled water system, but dry seasons are becoming longer and drier. Large areas of land to the north and east which drain into the national park have been set aside as preserves and wild-life management areas, but other areas regarded as crucial to Everglades National Park ecosystems remain in the hands of pri-vate owners, some with shopping-mall gleams in their eyes.

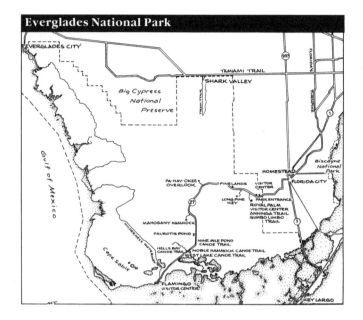

The continuing battle to save the East Everglades is among the hardest-fought conservation causes in U.S. history. By the dawn of the twenty-first century, some say, the everglades will be dead. See them now while you have the chance.

Everglades National Park
In the dry season, the everglades appear to be a vast plain of virgin grassland, the way Kansas must have looked before the first farmers arrived. But appearances are deceiving. The everglades, an ecosystem that exists nowhere else on earth except south Florida, are as inaccessible to man as the harshest desert. The "grass" is actually a primitive plant called sawgrass which livestock cannot eat. Its edges are as jagged as the name suggests, and its tips are needle-sharp silicate points; long after blades of sawgrass die and decay, the points remain on the ground like fine sand. The soil, even during the dry season when it looks like terra firma, is spongy and squishy. In the summer wet season, when 60 inches of rain (more than twice the annual rainfall of Seattle, Washington) fall in torrents, fresh water flows throughout the everglades in a river only a few inches deep but 50 miles or more wide, impossible for man or beast to cross on foot. During the Seminole Wars, the United States sent army expeditions in search of the Indians who lived on forested

islands in the everglades. Some never came back. Soldiers who
did return reported slogging through the everglades at the rate
of one mile a day until exhaustion turned them back. Even
today, no national park hiking trail ventures into the everglades
themselves. An hour's drive from downtown Miami, there is
not a single building or road. This is one of America's last great
wilderness areas.

You can see a grand vista of the everglades from the observation tower at **Pa-Hay-okee Overlook**, a turnout from the
park road. Your best close-up look at the sawgrass is from the
start of the Mahogany Hammock boardwalk.

Yet the everglades are only half the story. Many different
ecosystems fit together like puzzle pieces in Everglades
National Park. Minuscule changes in elevation make for drasti-
cally different life zones on the islands of dry ground that rise
from the everglades. Take the boardwalk through **Mahogany
Hammock**, one of many small, isolated hardwood stands.
Timbering on these hammocks was impossible before there
was a road, so in this hammock you'll find the oldest, largest-
known mahogany tree in the United States. The only known
example in the U.S. of a rare West Indian hand fern also used to
grow beside this boardwalk, but someone picked it. You can
see a large stand of dwarf cypress (leafless in winter, small but
over 100 years old) on the approach to Pa-hay-okee Overlook.
The best places to explore the higher, drier pinelands are the
short **Pinelands Nature Trail** and the 7-mile network of trails
around **Long Pine Key**. Most of the park's land mammals—
whitetail deer, raccoons, opossums, and possibly a Florida
panther—make their homes in this pine forest.

Almost half the land area of Everglades National Park is
covered by mangroves. These tough little trees can survive salt
water; notice how the red mangrove holds its trunk above
water level by using its curved roots as stilts and how the black
mangrove sends breathing tubes up from its roots to seek oxy-
gen above the water's surface. The maze of mangroves harbors
truly amazing numbers of large water birds—herons, egrets,
spoonbills, and even bald eagles—and the labyrinthine roots
shelter swarms of small fish, crabs, lobsters, and shrimp. Somewhere in this scrubby jungle may lurk the last wild crocodile in
the United States. Explore the mangroves on the boardwalk
trail from the **West Lake** parking lot. Deep in the mangroves are
open expanses of coastal prairie with desertlike vegetation—
cactus, yucca, and agave. To reach them, you must take one of
the long hiking trails from the Flamingo area (get details from
the visitors center there) such as the 4-mile **Snake Bight Trail**.

The two easiest and most popular trails, **Anhinga Trail**
(named for the water bird with a snakelike neck) and **Gumbo**

Limbo Trail (named for the unusual tree with peeling, coppery bark), follow a freshwater slough from Royal Palm Visitor Center near the park entrance and Long Pine Key campground. These are the most reliable places to see alligators. Once nearly extinct because of poaching, alligators can now be found in many freshwater lakes, springs, and rivers throughout Florida. Please do not feed, touch, or molest them. Alligators' brains are tiny, and while their instinctive fear of man makes them perfectly safe, if a 'gator loses that fear through too much human contact, he may have trouble telling the difference between tourists and lunch.

Boat Tours and Canoe Trips

Limited to the park road and boardwalks, you can only get a tantalizing sample of Everglades National Park. For a closer look at Florida Bay or the mangrove jungle, take a boat.

Several tour boats depart daily from the marina at Flamingo. A **Sunrise Sail** on Florida Bay leaves at 6:30 a.m. and returns at 8:00 a.m. for $10 per person; there is another two-hour **Florida Bay Cruise** by sailboat at 1:00 p.m., also for $10, and a **Sunset Sail** for $12 per person. **Backcountry Cruises** into the maze of waterways among the mangroves run at 9:00 a.m., 11:45 a.m., and 3:00 p.m. and cost $7.25 for adults, $3.60 for children ages 6 to 12. One-and-a-half-hour **Florida Bay Cruises** leave at 12:30 p.m., 2:30 p.m., and 5:15 p.m. for $5.50 per adult, $2.75 per child ages 6 to 12. An all-day tour to **Cape Sable**, the otherwise-inaccessible wilderness to the west of Flamingo, costs $35 per person.

Canoeing is the best way to enjoy this area. A two-hour guided **Sunrise Canoe Trip** on Florida Bay leaves daily at 6:00 a.m. and costs just $5 per person. No previous experience is necessary. The guides will teach you how to paddle a canoe in about five minutes. The water in the bay is not deep; you'll usually be able to touch the mucky bottom with your paddle. You'll see more birds than you can imagine, including pelicans, egrets and other large wading birds, and large flocks of skimmers that soar an inch above the water. You may glimpse a manta ray as it leaps from the water and lands with a loud slap. The sunrise is unforgettable. After that experience, can you resist renting a canoe to explore more on your own? Rent one for $10 per half day (daylight to 12:00 noon or noon to 5:00 p.m.) or $15 per full day, $20 cash deposit required. Rowboats rent at the marina store for the same price as canoes, and motorized skiffs rent for $40 per half day or $55 for a full day.

For sunrise sails and canoe trips, you must buy your tickets at the window in front of the marina store on the previous afternoon before 5:00 p.m. For other trips, you can get tickets up to five minutes before departure.

If boating in Everglades National Park turns out to be the high point of your Florida vacation (as it well may), and you've brought camping gear along, there is a well-marked 99-mile Wilderness Waterway from Flamingo to Everglades City. There is no current on most of the route, so you can canoe part or all of the way, in either direction, with ease. The trip takes about a week one way. If you don't have that much time, some other national park canoe trails to ask about at the marina are the Noble Hammock and Hell's Bay trails (3-4 miles, ½-day each) and the 8-mile, all-day West Lake Canoe Trail.

Itinerary Options

Morning and evening are the best times to see wildlife, while midday heat can be the biggest problem with exploring Everglades National Park. One solution is to take a sunrise boat or canoe trip, see the roadside boardwalks during the remainder of the morning, and leave the park for the afternoon to visit someplace cooler in the Homestead area.

Biscayne National Park, 21 miles east of the Everglades entrance (follow the big green signs), receives only 30,000 visitors a year (less than Walt Disney World gets in a single busy day). That's because virtually the entire park is underwater. If you enjoyed snorkeling in John Pennekamp Coral Reef State Park earlier, why not give it another try here? There are also glass-bottom boat tours as well as excursion boats to Elliot Key on the far side of the bay. For current snorkel, scuba, and boat tour information and prices, in English or Spanish, contact Biscayne National Park, P.O. Box 1369, Homestead, FL 33090-1369, (305) 247-PARK.

An equally good sightseeing option is the **Dade County Metro Zoo** at 12400 Coral Reef Drive, 251-0400. To get there, take Krome Avenue north from Homestead for about nine miles to Eureka Drive, turn right and follow Eureka to S.W. 134th Avenue, turn left there, and follow 134th as it curves around to S.W. 137th Avenue. Then turn right on Coral Reef Drive and you're there. The Metro Zoo is a cageless zoo. The animals run free on island habitats surrounded by moats; humans tour by walkway or monorail. Don't miss the giant "Wings of Asia" rain forest aviary. The zoo is open daily from 10:00 a.m. to 5:30 p.m., last admission at 4:00 p.m. Admission is $6 for adults, $3 for children ages 3 to 12. Monorail tickets (unlimited use all day) cost about $3 for adults, $2 for children.

Another sightseeing possibility in the Homestead area is **Coral Castle**, located at 286th Street and US 1, 248-6344. Edward Leedskalnin, a 97-pound Latvian immigrant, moved over 1,100 tons of rock without human assistance to build this palace for a young girl whom he loved obsessively. It took him 25 years, and the result has baffled scientists, engineers, and

scholars ever since it opened to the public in 1920. Hours are
9:00 a.m. to 9:00 p.m. daily. Admission is $7.25 for adults,
$4.50 for children ages 6 to 12.

The entrance fee you paid when you first entered Everglades
National Park is valid for seven days, so by presenting the
receipt you can reenter the park, explore some more along the
park road, and be back at Flamingo in time for a sunset cruise,
dinner at the lodge, and a relaxing evening.

THE TAMIAMI TRAIL

Many people who haven't been there expect Everglades
National Park to be a deep, dark swamp full of cypress trees and
orchids. By now, you know it's not. Today you'll see the real
cypress swamp, as well as the "Seminoles" most people know
about, who are actually Miccosukee Indians.

Suggested Schedule	
9:00 a.m.	Leave Flamingo.
10:30 a.m.	Exit Everglades National Park.
11:00 a.m.	Start driving the Tamiami Trail.
12:00 noon	Lunch at the Miccosukee Restaurant.
1:00 p.m.	Tour Shark Valley by bicycle or tram.
3:00 p.m.	See the Miccosukee Indian Village and take an airboat ride.
4:30 p.m.	Drive to a campground in Big Cypress National Preserve or a motel in Everglades City.

Travel Route: Homestead to Everglades City (90 miles)
After you leave Everglades National Park, turn left (north) on
Krome Avenue through Florida City and Homestead. Stay on
Krome (Highway 997) for 22 straight miles to the intersection
with US 41 and turn west. Once you're on US 41, getting lost is
practically impossible all the way to the Gulf Coast.

US 41, known as the Tamiami Trail (the melodic name stands
for Tampa-to-Miami) and built in 1928, was the first highway
across south Florida. Today there is also Highway 84 (75 cents
toll), officially known as the Everglades Parkway but always
called Alligator Alley, which runs from Fort Lauderdale to join
US 41 at Naples on the Gulf of Mexico. Dead straight, flat, and
fast, Alligator Alley is where big trucks roll like thunder past
signs that read, "Panther Habitat—Only 30 Left." Alligator Alley
attracts fast traffic away from the Tamiami Trail, leaving the old
route as unhurried as it must have been 50 years ago.

Past Big Cypress National Preserve, Everglades City is three
miles south of the Tamiami Trail on Highway 29.

Sightseeing Highlights
▲▲**Everglades National Park: Shark Valley**—Eighteen
miles after you turn west on US 41, you'll reach the Shark River
Slough, one of the best wildlife viewing areas of Everglades
National Park, with a 50-foot-tall observation tower at the end

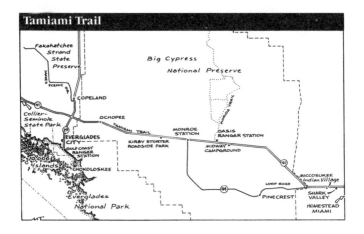

of the road commanding a fine view of the glades. Private vehicles are not allowed on the 15-mile road. A two-hour guided
tour by open-air tram costs $5 for adults, $4.50 for senior citizens, $2.50 for children; there is also a $3 per vehicle entrance
fee. Trams run daily at 9:00 a.m., 11:00 a.m., 1:00 p.m., and 3:00
p.m., with additional trips at 10:00 a.m. and 2:00 p.m. on Saturdays and Sundays. Reservations are recommended during the
winter months; call (305) 221-8455. Without a guide, you can
ride the route on a bicycle. If you didn't bring yours, you can
rent a bike at Shark Valley—first-come, first-served, $1.50 per
hour.

▲▲**Miccosukee Indian Village**—The Miccosukee people
speak a different language from the Muskogee-speaking Seminoles who live on the reservation near Lake Okeechobee. Both
groups were considered as one tribe, called Seminoles, until
recently when the federal government agreed to let them parti-
tion into separate reservations. The Miccosukee "village" one
mile past the Shark Valley entrance operates as a commercial
attraction, and it is the tribe's primary source of income. You'll
see chickee huts, the tribe's museum, demonstrations of
Seminole-style patchwork sewing and other arts and crafts, and
alligator wrestling. The village is open daily from 9:00 a.m. to
5:00 p.m. Admission is $5 for adults, $3.50 for senior citizens
and children. For an additional $6 apiece, an airboat will take
you on a 30-minute trip to a real, inhabited (by one family)
Indian hammock village on an island in the everglades.

▲▲**Big Cypress National Preserve**—This is the land of giant
cypress trees draped in Spanish moss and festooned with
orchids, bromeliads, and resurrection ferns. It's the kind of
deep, dark, mysterious forest where you'd expect alligators to

lurk—and they're here, along with panthers and black bears, deep in the primeval swamps where visitors rarely venture. Established in 1974 to protect part of the watershed for Everglades National Park, its national preserve designation was created specifically for this area, which could not be annexed to the national park because preexisting uses (such as airboat tours and hunting) would violate national park regulations and there is some private property inside the preserve.

Quick roadside stops along the Tamiami Trail are the modest visitors center at **Oasis Ranger Station** midway through the preserve and the **Kirby Storter Roadside Park** picnic area. If you have more time, drive the **Loop Road** scenic detour (State Road 94) that forks off to the left at the preserve boundary several miles past Shark Valley and rejoins the main route at Monroe Station, several miles west of Oasis Ranger Station.

If you'd like to hike into the cypress strands during the dry season, a network of unmarked hunters' trails from the far end of unmarked Midway Campground (see Camping below) makes for a good one-hour walk. The well-maintained Florida Trail starts at Oasis Ranger Station and goes north through the wilderness for 40 miles, all the way to Alligator Alley.

▲**Airboat Tours**—These flat-bottomed "swamp buggies" are no longer allowed in Everglades National Park, but several airboat companies along the Tamiami Trail operate tours into everglades areas of Big Cypress State Preserve. Half-hour trips typically cost $6 to $8, and half-day and all-day trips are also available. Other than those operated by the Miccosukee Indians, most airboat companies are in the Ochopee/Everglades City area. For information and reservations, contact **Wooten's Everglades Airboat Tours** (813-695-2781), **Donald McDowell's Airboat Guide Service** (813-695-2740), **Doug Dawley's Backcountry Airboat Guide Service** (813-695-3200), or **Tim Spaulding's Airboat & Swamp Buggy Guide Service** (813-695-2716 or 695-2682).

Food

The **Miccosukee Restaurant**, next door to the Miccosukee Information Center near the Indian Village and Shark Valley, specializes in Seminole and other Native American dishes such as catfish, fried frog legs, and Indian tacos. Prices are quite reasonable, and it's just about the only restaurant along the Tamiami Trail.

You'll find several inviting roadside picnic spots in Big Cypress National Preserve but no grocery stores. Stock up on food before leaving Homestead.

In addition to a supermarket, Everglades City has a good retail seafood market, **Johnson's Seafood**, where you can buy fresh fish, bluecrabs, stone crabs, oysters, shrimp, lobster, and frog legs. It is open until 6:00 p.m. You'll also find several restaurants there. Try the **Oyster House**. A long-established no-frills restaurant with good country cooking and daily specials is **Janes Restaurant** in Copeland, three miles north of the Tamiami Trail (the opposite direction from Everglades City) on Highway 29.

Lodging
Everglades City and its southern "suburb," Chokoloskee, have several motels that cater mainly to fishermen, including the **Sportsman's Club** (813-695-4224), the **Parkway Motel** (813-695-3261), and the **Blue Heron Motel** (813-695-2351). Typical rates are between $40 and $60.

Camping
Big Cypress National Preserve has several informal camping areas, none of them marked by signs. They are free but have no hookups. The best is **Midway Campground**, on the south side of the road about five miles east of the Oasis Ranger Station. Look for a "blue hole" quarry lake, which usually has a few RVs parked along the shore. Check out the trail that starts at the end of the blocked-off road beyond the south end of the lake.

    Big Cypress Trail Lakes Campground, just east of Ochopee, is the last privately owned, family-operated campground in Big Cypress National Preserve. It's small (40 RV sites with electric and water hookups, plus 25 tent sites), low-key, and somewhat old-fashioned, with a bass lake in the middle. This is one of the few places where you can actually hike through everglades sawgrass in the dry season; follow the airboat carrier tracks from the back of the campground. Rates are $12 per night.

    The best state park camping in the area is at **Collier-Seminole State Park**, on US 41, 16 miles past the turnoff to Everglades City. It's a large campground—130 sites—and costs about $15 a night.

Itinerary Options
There are 2,400 square miles of cypress swamp in south Florida—mostly inaccessible. To explore deep into a cypress strand by car, visit **Fakahatchee Strand State Preserve** on the Janes Scenic Drive, a former railroad bed that is now a dirt road. To get there, drive to Copeland (three miles north of the Tamiami Trail on Highway 29) and watch for the sign. This is the only place on earth where cypress and royal palm trees grow side by side. There are no facilities in the preserve, and you may find that you're the only visitor. The scenic drive is not a loop; drive out the same way you drove in.

Everglades City is the gateway to the **Ten Thousand Islands** area, a half-land, half-water mangrove maze, at the northwest corner of Everglades National Park. Canoes can be rented from NACT Everglades Outpost (813-695-4666), across from the park ranger station in Everglades City, for $12 per half day, $18 per full day. Concessioners also operate scenic boat tours into the Ten Thousand Islands from the national park docks between Everglades City and Chokoloskee; for current schedules and prices, call (813)-695-2591 or (800) 445-7724.

CORKSCREW SWAMP AND SANIBEL ISLAND

Today's itinerary offers a triple feature of outstanding sights in the Fort Myers area. You'll get a close-up look at a primeval cypress swamp teeming with alligators and wading birds, visit the spot where Thomas Edison invented the swimming pool, and stroll along the best seashell-hunting beach in America.

Suggested Schedule

8:30 a.m.	Drive to Corkscrew Swamp.
9:00 a.m.	Visit Corkscrew Swamp.
10:30 a.m.	Drive to Fort Myers.
12:00 noon	Visit the Edison Winter Home.
3:00 p.m.	Drive to Sanibel Island.
3:30 p.m.	Find your two seashells.
5:00 p.m.	Check into your accommodations or drive to your campground.

Travel Route: Everglades City to Corkscrew Swamp (57 miles) to Fort Myers (52 miles)
From the intersection of US 41 (the Tamiami Trail) and Highway 29 (the road from Everglades City), continue north on Highway 29 for 20 miles, cross Alligator Alley, and continue for 10 more miles. Watch for State Road 858 on your left, which takes you straight west for 16 miles and then dead-ends into State Road 846. Turn right (north) and go 5 miles. Immediately after the road curves east, watch for the turnoff to Corkscrew Swamp (State Road 849) on your left.

When you leave Corkscrew Swamp, turn east (left) on State Road 846 and follow it all the way to Immokalee, a distance of 14 miles. Turn left on Highway 82 westbound and stay on it for as far as it goes—36 miles, straight into downtown Fort Myers, where it becomes Anderson Boulevard, then veers half-left and becomes McGregor Boulevard, leading directly to the Edison Winter Home.

Sightseeing Highlights

▲▲▲ **Corkscrew Swamp Sanctuary**—If you stop to visit a cypress swamp only once in your life, make it this one. The 11,000-acre refuge was acquired by the National Audubon Society in the late 1950s to protect the habitat of the nation's largest colony of wood storks, an endangered species. It contains one of the last virgin strands of giant bald cypress in Florida. Some

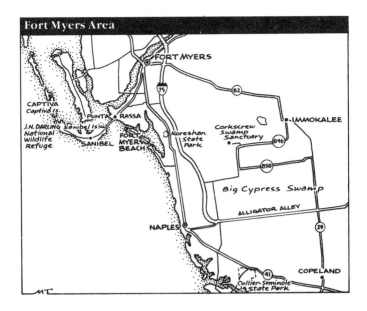

Fort Myers Area

of the largest trees are 500 years old. This is the best place in the cypress swamps to watch wildlife. As you near the last, best part of the 1¾-mile boardwalk, watch the muddy "lettuce ponds." Fish concentrate there as the swamp water level drops during the winter dry season, and many water birds and alligators gather to eat them. (In the summer wet season, the area is under as much as 4½ feet of water.) Pause to watch the large bird feeder near the visitors center and notice some of the smaller birds that also inhabit this forest, among them, perhaps, the painted bunting, the most colorful bird in North America. Corkscrew Swamp Sanctuary is open daily from 9:00 a.m. to 5:00 p.m. Admission is $4 for Audubon Society members, $5 for adult nonmembers, $2 for students, children under age 6 free.

▲▲▲**Edison Winter Home**—In 1885, six years after he invented the electric light, Thomas Edison collapsed from exhaustion. Doctors warned that he would soon die unless he moved to a warmer climate. (If you're escaping from winter up north, you probably know that feeling.) So Edison moved to Fort Myers and spent his winters here for 46 years.

In the subtropics, Edison's inventive genius seems to have turned in other directions than the electrical technologies he is usually remembered for. His home and guest house were the first prefabricated buildings in America, crafted in Maine and moved here in pieces aboard four schooners. He built the first swimming pool in Florida and the original underground irrigation system. He puttered in his giant "garden," growing over 6,000 species of exotic trees, vines, and plants from around the world and devising a way to make synthetic rubber from a 14-foot-tall strain of goldenrod weed he had developed.

Edison's house and laboratory are just as he left them. The museum across the street is full of Edison inventions and memorabilia. The Edison Winter Home is located at 2530 McGregor Boulevard. It is open Monday through Saturday from 9:00 a.m. to 4:00 p.m., Sundays from 12:30 p.m. to 4:00 p.m., closed Thanksgiving and Christmas Day. Guided tours run continuously. Admission is $4 for adults, $1 for children ages 6 to 12.

▲**Sanibel and Captiva Islands**—In an uneasy compromise between conservation and development, resorts, condominiums, and shopping malls fill about half the area of these crescent-shaped islands southwest of Fort Myers, while the other half is preserved in its natural state within the 5,000-acre J. N. "Ding" Darling National Wildlife Refuge, year-round home to 43 species of birds and migration stop for over 200 other species. View the refuge from the road on top of the 5-mile mosquito control dike. Farther out in open water, watch for leaping dolphins. Sanibel and Captiva are renowned for the best seashell hunting in Florida. In fact, these days beachcombing here is so popular that you're only allowed to remove two shells per person. The best place to search is Turner Beach on the pass between the two islands, and the best time is when the tide is going out.

To reach the islands from Thomas Edison's house, continue south on McGregor Boulevard for 15 miles to the Sanibel Causeway. Cross the causeway ($3 round-trip toll) and you're on Sanibel Island.

Food

In Fort Myers, most of the moderately priced restaurants are south of downtown along US 41 (Cleveland Avenue—turn south where Anderson Avenue becomes McGregor Boulevard). Try **Morrison's Cafeteria**, 3057 South Cleveland Avenue; **Casa Lupita** (Mexican food), 12148 South Cleveland Avenue; or **Bill Knapps** at the intersection of US 41 and Cypress Lake Drive. (Cypress Lake Drive will take you west to McGregor Boulevard, which goes to Sanibel Island, without returning to downtown.)

Sanibel and Captiva have over three dozen restaurants. If you feel that you deserve a splurge dinner after three days in the wilderness, order it at the **Thistle Lodge Restaurant** at Casa Ybel Resort, 2255 West Gulf Drive. Call 472-3145 for reservations. Dinner hours are Monday through Saturday from 5:30 to 9:00 p.m. Luncheon is also served seven days a week. The specialties are Cajun and Creole dishes. Expect to spend about $30 per person. **The Snooty Fox**, 2075 Periwinkle Place (in the Periwinkle Place Shopping Center), 472-2525, claims to be "Sanibel's only affordable family restaurant," and they're probably right.

Dining is more affordable in Fort Myers Beach. Try the **Pelican**, 3040 Estero Boulevard, 463-6139. Seafood is served in seafaring surroundings overlooking the Gulf of Mexico. Expect to spend $15 per person. Dinner is served daily from 4:30 to 10:00 p.m. (closed during September). An old favorite on the beach is **The Mucky Duck**, 2500 Estero Boulevard, 463-5519, serving reasonably priced dinners from 5:00 to 9:30 p.m. daily.

Lodging

Sanibel and Captiva have become trendy recently, with accordingly upscale accommodation rates. Still, it's been a while since you've seen a beach resort on this itinerary, so why not spend the extra few dollars? Early morning is a fine time to beachcomb or bird-watch. Major resorts here have minimum stay requirements of as much as a week, but any of the apartment motels along Gulf Drive will do nicely and cost less. At **Song of the Sea**, 863 East Gulf Drive, (813) 472-2220, apartments with kitchens rent for about $130 to $150 a night and up during high season (Christmas holidays and February through mid-April); January costs less (about $90) and November even less (about $80). **Jolly Roger's Resort Motel**, 3287 West Gulf Drive, (813) 472-1700, also rents apartments, with winter rates from $75 per night for efficiencies to $125 for suites. The **Gallery Motel**, 541 East Gulf Drive, (813) 472-1400, has apartments in the same price range. All are on the beach, all have heated pools, none accept pets.

Fort Myers has name-brand motels in all price ranges, with some winter rates as low as $45 a night. The motel strip is both north and south of town on Cleveland Avenue (US 41).

Camping

The most interesting place to camp in the area is **Koreshan State Historic Park** in Estero, 20 miles south of Fort Myers on US 41. The 60-site state campground adjoins a restoration of the utopian religious commune built here in 1894 by Cyrus Reed Teed, who advocated sexual abstinence and believed that the earth surrounded the sun. The park also has nature trails. No pets.

You'll find several RV parks around nearby Fort Myers Beach. Try the **San Carlos RV Trailer Park**, 18701 San Carlos Boulevard, (813) 466-3133, which has sites on small offshore islands in Hurricane Bay for about $20 a night.

SARASOTA

Circus promoter John Ringling put Sarasota on the map and shaped the town's peculiar character. The estate he built here is a three-ring museum complete with a living-room pipe organ, a circus calliope, and millions of dollars worth of art. You'll want to spend all day here—but leave in time to reach St. Petersburg ahead of the rush hour.

Suggested Schedule

9:00 a.m.	Drive to Sarasota.
10:30 a.m.	Visit the Ringling Museums.
3:00 p.m.	Drive to St. Petersburg.
3:30 p.m.	Check into your accommodations in St. Petersburg Beach for two nights or occupy a campsite at Fort DeSoto County Park.
4:00 p.m.	Spend the rest of the day at the beach.

Travel Route: Fort Myers to Sarasota (75 miles) to St. Petersburg (30 miles)

From anywhere in the Fort Myers area, take the most direct marked route to Interstate 75, about 5 miles inland, and go 75 miles north on the interstate to Sarasota. Take the University Parkway (Airport) exit. Head west until you reach North Washington Boulevard, turn south (left) there and then west (left) on De Soto. Follow De Soto to the waterfront and you'll find yourself at the Ringling Museums.

On leaving the Ringling estate, go north on the Tamiami Trail (US 41) through Bradenton and across the Manatee River, then follow US 19 to Interstate 275 and the Sunshine Skyway, the 11-mile bridge over Tampa Bay ($.50 per axle toll) with its high arched central span that even the largest ships can pass under. (In 1980, a cargo ship crashed into the original, somewhat lower bridge, the wreckage of which parallels this new one, killing 35 motorists.) At the north end of the causeway, turn west on the Pinellas Bayway ($.50 toll) to reach St. Petersburg Beach or Fort DeSoto Park. To reach St. Petersburg's downtown waterfront, stay on 275 for three more exits and take Fifth Avenue eastbound to the art museum and municipal fishing pier.

Sightseeing Highlights

Ringling Museums—John and Rudolf Ringling began as penniless Wisconsin farmboys and parlayed a juggling act into the

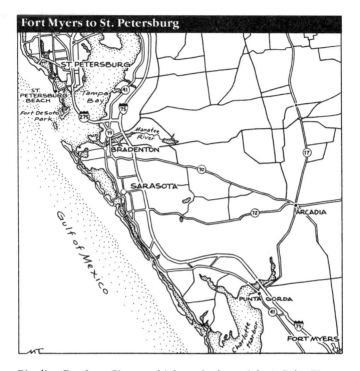

Fort Myers to St. Petersburg

Ringling Brothers Circus, which made them rich. At John Ringling's estate, you'll see just how rich. **C'ad'zan**, the 30-room
mansion he built as a $1.5 million gift for his wife, is a replica of
the Renaissance Doge's Palace in Venice, Italy. Italian artisans
handcrafted the ornate stonework of the mansion and vast
patios, importing fine materials from all over the world. There
are mansions of the rich and famous all over Florida, but this is
probably the only one with a pipe organ in the living room.

The task of decorating his palace so captured Ringling's
imagination that he became a serious, knowledgeable collector
of European art and quickly ran out of wall space. To house the
collection, he built a replica of a Renaissance villa in Florence,
Italy. The **John and Mable Ringling Museum of Art**, now the
Florida state art museum, focuses on works from fourteenth-
through eighteenth-century Western Europe, emphasizing the
baroque period, and includes what many consider to be the
finest collection in existence of Pierre Paul Rubens's paintings.
The inner courtyard of the art museum is set with full-size
reproductions of famous statues, such as a bronze cast of
Michelangelo's *David*.

The **Circus Galleries**, a more modest building that hardly hints at the array of unique items inside, shows off circus wagons, circus costumes, miniature circuses, a steam calliope, posters, and other memorabilia of "the Greatest Show on Earth." The fourth building on the estate is the **Asolo Theater**, a replica of a rococo-style Italian theater of the eighteenth century, where Florida's state repertory company presents plays from December through July, with both matinee and evening performances. For current showbill information and reservations, call (813) 355-5137.

The Ringling Museums are open daily from 10:00 a.m. to 6:00 p.m. (until 10:00 p.m. on Thursdays). Lunch is available there. Admission to all the buildings is $4.50 for adults, $1.75 for children ages 6 to 12; admission is free on Saturdays, as Ringling stipulated in his will.

Other Sarasota Museums—Ringling's presence shaped the city's character, an odd blend of culture-consciousness and showmanship that has encouraged other offbeat museums. Two collectors' dreams-come-true are **Bellm's Cars and Music of Yesterday** (170 classic cars and 2,000 music devices, 5500 North Tamiami Trail, open until 6:00, $4.95 for adults, $2.25 for children ages 6 to 16) and the **Lionel Train and Seashell Museum** (8184 North Tamiami Trail, open until 5:00 p.m., seashell exhibits free, small admission charge to see the electric trains).

Sarasota also prides itself on its downtown "art district," with galleries scattered along Main Street between the 1300 and 1900 blocks.

Food

For dinner in St. Petersburg Beach, **Summer's Landing** at 5100 Gulf Boulevard, 360-4949, is one of many good, casual, reasonably priced ($8 and up) seafood restaurants along the beach. Hours are 11:30 a.m. to 10:00 p.m. daily. Another is **Silas Dent's**, 5501 Gulf Boulevard, 360-6961, open daily from 5:00 p.m. to 10:00 p.m. (until 11:00 p.m. on weekend nights).

A very expensive restaurant where you can eat beluga caviar and sip uncommon wines to the strains of harp music is the King Charles Room in St. Petersburg Beach's long-time landmark hotel, **Don CeSar Beach Resort**, 3400 Gulf Boulevard. Call 360-1881 for dinner reservations. You can visit another top-of-the-line beach hotel and dine in a lower price range (around $20) at Palm Court in the **Tradewinds**, 5500 Gulf Boulevard. For dinner reservations, call 367-6461. The restaurant also serves breakfast.

Lodging

St. Petersburg Beach offers beachfront accommodations with an exceptionally wide range of rates. The best prices (winter rates often start at $50 or $60, off-season rates as low as $30) are often found at the apartment motels; try the **Holiday Shores Motel**, 3860 Gulf Boulevard, (813) 367-1967, or the **Palm Crest Motel**, 3848 Gulf Beach Boulevard, (813) 360-9327.

Finer accommodations, in the $150-and-up range, include the **Don CeSar Beach Resort**, 3400 Gulf Boulevard, (813) 360-1881, a pink palace from the 1920s (F. Scott Fitzgerald's favorite) that has been undergoing extensive renovation, and the **Tradewinds**, 5500 Gulf Boulevard, (813) 367-6461 or (800) 237-0707, a new all-suite resort with old Florida landscaping—gazebos, white latticework, and canals where gondolas and swans glide.

Slightly lower-priced beachfront motel accommodations ($40 and up) can be found on Treasure Island, farther north along Gulf Boulevard.

The **St. Petersburg International Hostel** (AAIH) in the historic Detroit Hotel, 215 Central Avenue in downtown St. Petersburg, within walking distance of the Salvador Dali Museum and the waterfront, offers dormitory accommodations at $10 a night and a few plain private rooms starting at $18. Call (813) 822-4095. There are a restaurant, pub, and dance club on the premises. No curfew.

Also downtown, also historic, but at the other end of the price spectrum, is the newly renovated **Heritage**, the city's grand hotel from the 1920s. It is located at 234 Third Avenue North, between the Museum of Fine Arts and the Salvador Dali Museum. For rate information and reservations, call (813) 822-4814.

Camping

Fort DeSoto County Park has beaches, an old fort from the Spanish-American War, a wildlife refuge, and a large campground. This is the place where Ponce de Leon landed on his second trip to Florida in 1521 and was fatally wounded in a battle with local Indians. To get there, turn south at the golf course midway between Interstate 275 and St. Petersburg Beach, then follow the Pinellas Bayway (State Road 679) south as far as it goes—9 miles—to Mullet Key. Turn right on Anderson Boulevard to the park. Sites cost $12 a night. No pets.

St. Petersburg KOA, 5400 95th Street N., (813) 392-2233, is located on the west side of town, not far from the St. Petersburg Beach Causeway. To get there from I-275, exit north of downtown at 38th Avenue. Go west on 38th for 5½ miles, then veer

right onto Tyrone (which becomes Bay Pines) and follow it to
95th Street, where you turn right and go another half-mile. This
is an RV "resort" along a bayou, with shade trees, a fishing
dock, boats and canoes, and a hot tub. Sites cost about $26 a
night.

ST. PETERSBURG

Spend the morning at the beach or explore the St. Petersburg waterfront. The Salvador Dali Museum opens at noon. When you've had enough of madness, drive over to Bradenton to meet a friendly manatee and maybe see a laser light show.

Suggested Schedule

9:00 a.m.	Back to the beach or wander the waterfront in downtown St. Petersburg.
11:00 a.m.	Eat lunch early.
12:00 noon	Visit the Salvador Dali Museum.
2:30 p.m.	Cross the Sunshine Causeway to Bradenton.
3:00 p.m.	Visit the South Florida Museum.
Evening	If it's a weekend night, see the laser light show at the South Florida Museum.

Sightseeing Highlights

▲▲**St. Petersburg's Beaches**—In addition to the free municipal beach at St. Petersburg Beach and those around Fort DeSoto Park (see Day 16 Travel Route and Camping for details), a popular beach that locals consider the best in the area is Pass-a-Grille Beach on the point south of St. Petersburg Beach.

▲▲**St. Petersburg's Bayfront**—The downtown waterfront has seen extensive renovation during the 1980s. Today, it is a pleasant district of museums, galleries, and boutiques, with a bayfront park and public fishing pier. **The Museum of Fine Arts** at 255 Beach Drive N.E. (corner of Beach Drive and Second Avenue North) is one of Florida's finest art museums. The diverse collections include originals of several familiar paintings by French artists like Monet, Renoir, and Gaugin. The art museum is open Tuesday through Saturday from 10:00 a.m. to 5:00 p.m., Sundays from 1:00 p.m. to 5:00 p.m., closed Mondays. Donations are accepted.

Nearby, at 335 Second Avenue N.E. adjacent to the fishing pier, is the **St. Petersburg Historical Museum**. Exhibits include a history of baseball and spring training. The history museum is open the same hours as the Museum of Fine Arts. Admission is $2 for adults, $1.50 for senior citizens, and $.50 for children under 12. **Great Explorations** is a new, fun "hands-on" museum at 1120 Fourth Street South, across the street from the Salvador Dali Museum. Kids love it. Hours are Monday through Saturday from 10:00 a.m. to 5:00 p.m. and Sundays from 1:00 p.m. to 5:00 p.m. **The Pier**, the strange building that

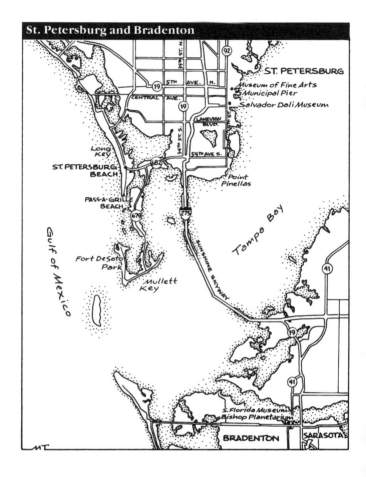

St. Petersburg and Bradenton

looks like a pyramid balanced on its point overlooking the
water at the end of Second Avenue N.E., has specialty shops,
restaurants, and bay views galore.

▲▲▲ **Salvador Dali Museum**—Visiting Ringling's museums
yesterday may have suggested new insights into the relationship
between showmanship and the fine arts. Today, you can see
both run amok in this museum, which contains over 1,200 Dali
works valued at upwards of $100 million, all donated to the state
of Florida by a collector from Cleveland, Ohio. It's the largest
collection anywhere of paintings, prints, sculptures, and unclas-
sifiably strange objects by the late Spanish surrealist who
proved once and for all that art and madness (and publicity) go

together like a horse and carriage. It's all so bizarre that you, too, may feel a little crazy after seeing it. The gift shop contains a great selection of Dali postcards, posters, books, and T-shirts. The museum is open Tuesday through Saturday from 12:00 noon to 5:00 p.m. and Sundays from 12:00 noon to 5:00 p.m., closed Mondays. Admission is $3.50 for adults, $2.25 for senior citizens and students, free for children under age 8. It is located at 1000 Third Street South in Poynter Park on the downtown waterfront and has free off-street parking.

▲▲**South Florida Museum**—Of the many museums in the Bradenton/St. Petersburg/Tampa area, we especially like this one because it provides the best chance you'll ever have to get a close-up look at a live manatee ("sea cow") and wonder how early sailors could have mistaken them for mermaids. (Even if you're lucky enough to spot one of these endangered aquatic relatives of the elephant swimming wild in a Florida river, all you're likely to see is its bulbous, whiskery nose poking up out of murky water.) Snooty, the museum's mascot, is the oldest living manatee born in captivity—in 1948.

Besides Snooty, the museum's eclectic exhibits include life-size dioramas of Indian and pioneer life, a re-created Spanish colonial courtyard and chapel, antique medical and surgical devices, planetarium shows, and collections of minerals, seashells, and Civil War memorabilia.

The South Florida Museum is open Tuesday through Friday from 10:00 a.m. to 5:00 p.m., Saturday and Sunday from 12:00 noon to 5:00 p.m., closed Mondays. Admission is $3 for adults, $2 for students, free for children under school age. The museum is located at 201 Tenth Street West in Bradenton; to get there, retrace yesterday's route across the Sunshine Causeway and south on US 19. Immediately after you cross the bridge over the Manatee River into Bradenton, turn right on Manatee Avenue to Tenth Street. The museum is on your right.

Food
In downtown St. Petersburg, the best place to look for lunch is **The Pier**, where, besides a good Colombian restaurant, you'll find a bakery and a deli that sell everything you might want for a picnic in the park.

Nightlife
Bishop Planetarium at the South Florida Museum in Bradenton presents *Laser Fantasies* on Friday and Saturday nights at 9:00 p.m., 10:30 p.m., and 12:00 midnight and Sunday evenings at 6:00 p.m. These are uncompromising, high-energy rock light shows featuring different music each week. A gentler, family-oriented light show, *Laser Dreams*, plays Sunday afternoons at

4:30 p.m. Admission to either show is $3.50 for adults, $2.75 for children under 13. Bishop Planetarium's staff includes some of the most innovative laser artists and special effects technicians in the planetarium world, and to a much greater extent than in most other laser shows, the "visual music" is performed live using synthesizer keyboards along with control panels and computers. Even if you've seen laser shows before, *Laser Fantasies* will knock your socks off! The South Florida Museum's rooftop observatory, which houses a 12½-inch telescope, is open several evenings each month for public stargazing. Call the museum at 746-4131 for current laser program information and observatory schedules.

The Gray Line riverboat ***Belle of St. Petersburg*** offers moonlight cruises around Tampa Bay on Wednesdays, Fridays, and Saturdays, departing at 7:00 from the tour boat dock at 401 Second Avenue N.E. (downtown across from the yacht basin and the big pink Vinoy Hotel) and returning around 10:00 p.m. The fare, which includes a hearty buffet dinner and wine, is $18 for adults, $10.50 for children under age 10. For reservations, call 823-1665 or 823-8171.

THE PINELLAS SUNCOAST TO OCALA

The towns along the Pinellas Suncoast are a mix of golf courses, lovely homes, and Old World Greek charm. Today's route offers chances to see a spring teeming with fish and another one full of mermaids, but the day's top sight is the remains of a mysterious lost Indian civilization.

Suggested Schedule

9:00 a.m.	Drive up the Pinellas Suncoast. Visit your choice of sightseeing highlights en route— Tarpon Springs, Weeki Wachee, or Homosassa Springs.
12:00 noon	Visit the Crystal River Indian mounds.
2:00 p.m.	Drive to Ocala.
3:30 p.m.	Find a motel in Ocala for two nights or head into the national forest in search of a campground.

Travel Route: St. Petersburg to Ocala (124 miles)
From downtown St. Petersburg or Interstate 275, get on Fifth Avenue North and follow the US 19 Alternate signs west. The route veers right to become Tyrone Boulevard, then Bay Pines Boulevard; then it turns north to become Seminole Boulevard. At Largo, steer left on Bay Drive and then right on Clearwater Largo Road (still following US 19 Alt.). The route reaches the coast in Clearwater and follows it north to Tarpon Springs, a total distance of 33 miles from downtown St. Petersburg. Traffic is slow along this route, but the homes are lovely. A few miles north of Tarpon Springs, you'll join US 19, leave the developed area of the coast, and drive 52 miles north to Crystal River, passing Weeki Wachee and Homosassa Springs along the way. Follow the signs to Crystal River State Archaeological Site.

After seeing the Indian mounds, continue north on US 19/98 to Inglis, turn east (right) on County Road 40, and drive 14 miles to Dunnellon. Turn north (left) on US 41 and go 5 miles, then northeast (right) on Highway 40 for another 20 miles to Ocala.

Sightseeing Highlights
▲**Tarpon Springs**—Greek immigrant sponge divers who had been working in Tampa Bay began moving here around the turn of the century. Although the market for natural sponges has long since dried up, this small community still adds an ethnic

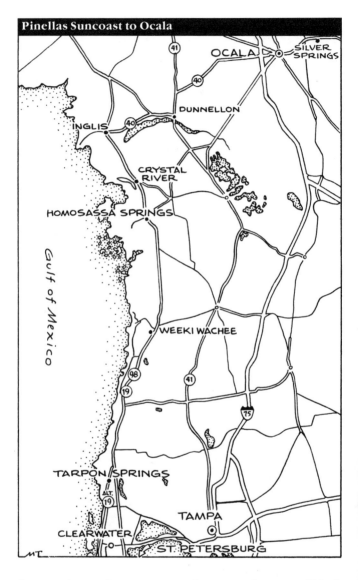

Pinellas Suncoast to Ocala

flavor to the Pinellas Suncoast. In the center of town you'll find
shops that sell souvenir sponges, a few boats that gather them,
and picturesque, unemployed-looking locals, as well as Greek
restaurants and pastry shops. The most interesting sight is Saint
Nicholas Greek Orthodox church, a replica of Saint Sophia's.

The church is open to the public from 2:00 p.m. to 5:00 p.m. daily. Donations are accepted.

▲**Florida's Weeki Wachee**—Young women wearing bright-colored fishtails perform underwater at this famous old-time tourist attraction. (It's your only chance on this itinerary to see mermaids and wonder how early sailors could have mistaken these lovely creatures for sea cows.) The theme park also has a river cruise, a nature trail, bird shows, and a petting zoo. The park is open daily from 9:00 a.m. to 6:00 p.m., with mermaid shows hourly from 11:00 a.m. to 5:00 p.m. Admission is $8.95 for adults, $5.50 for children ages 3 to 11.

▲**Homosassa Springs Nature World**—Another natural spring turned tourist attraction, this one teems with both salt-water and freshwater fish, which you can watch from a glass "fishbowl" observatory that lets you walk underwater. Other attractions include a nature trail, a river cruise, a petting zoo, and an alligator lagoon. The park also has a rehabilitation center for injured and orphaned manatees. It is open daily from 9:00 a.m. to 5:30 p.m. Admission is $6.95 for adults, $5.60 for senior citizens, and $3.95 for children ages 3 to 11.

▲▲**Crystal River State Archaeological Site**—An ancient Indian civilization thrived here from 200 B.C. to A.D. 1400 but had disappeared by the time the first Europeans reached Florida. If the shapes and arrangement of temple mounds here remind you of the great stone pyramids in Mexico, it's probably no coincidence. The Crystal River people had trade relations with the Toltecs as well as with northern Indian groups all the way to Illinois; you can look at the evidence, in the form of artifacts excavated from this ceremonial center, in the visitors center's museum displays. Stelae (carved stone columns), the only ones north of Mexico, suggest that these Indians also had contact with the Mayan culture of the Yucatán. The steep, squarish mounds were once stuccoed with clay and had palm-thatched wooden temples on top. Other mounds were built for burials and for disposal of trash, including tons of seashells. An astronomical clock, the intricate designs on the central sun-stone still barely visible, is located in the far corner of the park. The grounds are open daily from 8:00 a.m. to sundown. The visitors center/museum is open Thursday through Monday from 9:00 a.m. to 5:00 p.m. and charges $.50 per person admission. The site is 2 ½ miles west of the highway on clearly marked State Park Road.

Food and Lodging
Motels and restaurants seem to be the main industry in Ocala (pop. 40,000). Major chain motels and franchise restaurants cluster along Highway 40 (Silver Springs Boulevard) where it meets Interstate 75. Continue on Silver Springs Boulevard

through downtown, and on the east side you'll find a strip of older ma-and-pa motels offering remarkably low rates, many for $25 to $30 per night. Don't worry about advance reservations; just watch for vacancy signs and take your pick.

One of the finest restaurants in Ocala is **Spencer's 1890 House**, near downtown at 917 East Silver Springs Boulevard. American and Chinese dishes range in price all the way from about $7 to about $20. Hours are daily from 11:30 a.m. to 2:00 a.m. (until 9:00 p.m. on Sundays). Call 622-1232 for reservations. For a plainer ambience and good, low-priced food, **Morrison's Cafeteria**, at 1600 East Silver Springs Boulevard, is open daily from 11:00 a.m. to 8:30 p.m.

Camping
There are sixteen campgrounds in Ocala National Forest. The easiest to reach, and the most popular, is the 78-site campground at **Juniper Springs**, one of tomorrow's sightseeing highlights, 28 miles east of Ocala on Highway 40. The camping fee is $7.

A more secluded, primitive campground in the same area is on the shores of **Lake Eaton**, 19 miles east of Ocala on Highway 40, then 4¼ miles north on County Road 314 Alt., ½ mile east on Forest Road 79A, and one mile north on Forest Road 96. There are outhouses but no drinking water. Camping here, as at many other small fishing lakes hidden away in the national forest, is free. To find more, stop at the Ocala National Forest ranger station on Highway 40 for a free "National Forests in Florida Recreation Area Directory" and a $1 forest map.

The only drawback to national forest campgrounds is that they do not have hookups. Occasionally in winter months, Ocala nights can be chilly. If you need a place to plug in your heater, try the **Ocala/Silver Springs KOA**, located at 3200 S.W. 38th Avenue, off College Road just west of Interstate 75 (exit 68). Rates are about $19 a night.

OCALA NATIONAL FOREST AND CROSS CREEK

Many visitors to the Ocala area are content to spend their day at Silver Springs, the oldest commercial tourist attraction in Florida. An equally attractive choice is to discover the hidden lakes and springs of Ocala National Forest, an excursion you can easily combine with a visit to Marjorie Kinnan Rawlings's home, the setting for the classic book and recent movie, *Cross Creek*.

Suggested Schedule

9:00 a.m.	Drive to Juniper Springs.
10:00 a.m.	Swim in the springs or paddle a canoe.
12:00 noon	Picnic.
1:00 p.m.	Continue your driving tour of Ocala National Forest.
3:00 p.m.	Visit Cross Creek.
5:00 p.m.	Return to Ocala.

[Alternate plan: All day at Silver Springs]

Travel Route: Ocala National Forest and Cross Creek (103 miles)

For an all-day joyride through the national forest, including swimming or hiking at Juniper Springs and a side trip to Cross Creek, from Ocala proceed east on Highway 40 (Silver Springs Boulevard) past Silver Springs, 25 miles to Juniper Springs.

When you leave Juniper Springs, continue east on Highway 40 a short distance to the intersection with Highway 19. Turn north (left) and drive 15 miles, passing Lake George and the private Silver Glenn Springs Recreation Area on your right, to Salt Springs. There, turn west (left) on County Road 316 past Lake Kerr. You leave the national forest as you cross the Oklawaha River at Eureka. Continue west to County Road 200-A (US 301 Business Route), turn north (right), and go about 2½ miles to join US 301. Follow the main highway through Citra to Island Grove, about 3½ miles, and turn west (left) on County Road 325 for about 4 miles to Cross Creek. Watch for the Marjorie Kinnan Rawlings Home on your left near where the road veers north.

To return from Cross Creek to Ocala, backtrack to US 301, turn south (right), and drive 20 miles. You'll enter Ocala on Pine Avenue, which intersects Silver Springs Boulevard downtown.

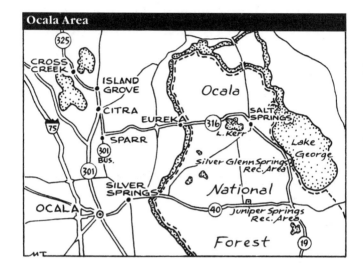

Sightseeing Highlights

▲▲**Silver Springs**—Silver Springs has the distinction of being
Florida's oldest commercial tourist attraction, established in
1890. These artesian springs are the largest in the world, with a
combined flow of over one billion gallons of water per day.
Glass-bottom tour boats were invented for use here. While
modern versions of the underwater viewing boats are still the
center of attention, Silver Springs has added an eclectic assortment of other things to see and do—enough to keep you busy
all day and justify the steep admission charge. There are a jungle
cruise ride (unlike Disney's, the African animals here are alive),
an exotic reptile show, a deer park, a classic car collection, and a
doll collection as well as lush gardens, cute shops, and restaurants. Silver Springs is open daily from 9:00 a.m. to 5:30 p.m.
(entrance closes at 4:00 p.m.). Admission is $13.95 for adults
and $6.95 for children ages 3 to 11.

▲▲**Ocala National Forest**—This 380,000-acre woodland
was the first national forest to be established east of the Missis-
sippi River. It is the southernmost national forest in the United
States, and it attracts more recreation visitors each year than any
other. Scenic features of Ocala National Forest include large
springs and over 600 lakes. The most accessible place for
daytrips to the national forest is Juniper Springs Recreation
Area, where Juniper Springs and Fern Hammock Springs create
a combined flow of 20 million gallons a day. You can swim in
Juniper Springs pool (water temperature is 72 degrees year-
round) or rent a canoe (35 are available rent at the grocery store)

and explore the spring runs. You can reserve a canoe by calling (904) 625-2808 between 9:00 a.m. and midnight. On weekdays, you should find canoes available without reservations. For hiking, the 68-mile Ocala National Recreation Trail crosses the Juniper Springs entrance road and runs north for the next 7 miles through the Juniper Prairie Wilderness. Wander as far as you like.

Salt Springs Recreation Area is another group of freshwater springs, with a flow of 52 million gallons a day. On the edge of Lake George, it is a popular boating and fishing area. Canoes are for rent at the marina. A trail from the parking lot leads to another part of the Ocala Trail.

Both recreation areas open their gates at 8:00 a.m. and, for camper security, lock them at 8:00 p.m.

▲**Marjorie Kinnan Rawlings Home**—In the small village of Cross Creek is another writer's house. Its only resemblance to the Hemingway House in Key West is that both contain typewriters. When Ms. Rawlings, the wife of a New York publisher, abandoned her marriage and social standing to live, write, and grow oranges in rural Florida, Cross Creek was little more than a fish camp; only three families lived there, and the Rawlings Home was a four-room cottage. She wrote her 1938 Pulitzer Prize-winning novel *The Yearling*, her 1941 best-selling memoir *Cross Creek*, and many other books here. Her portrayals of life in the backwoods were so vividly accurate that one of her neighbors sued her in a landmark invasion-of-privacy case. Since the motion picture version of *Cross Creek*, starring Academy Award-winner Mary Steenburgen as Ms. Rawlings, was released in 1983, the number of visitors to the area has doubled. The village has grown (there are now a restaurant and a lodge), but it's still a pretty, out-of-the-way little place. The Marjorie Kinnan Rawlings House, now a State Historic Site, is open from 9:00 a.m. to 5:00 p.m. Guided tours are given Mondays and Thursday through Sunday between the hours of 10:00 a.m. and 4:30 p.m. Admission is $1 per person.

CEDAR KEY AND MANATEE SPRINGS

Cedar Key ranked among Florida's most important port cities a century ago, when Miami was a mosquito-infested mangrove jungle. Today it's a small, quiet hideaway that will give you a sample of the state's little-known "hidden coast." Later, drive to pretty Manatee Springs, a perfect camping spot 'way down upon the Suwannee River.

Suggested Schedule

9:00 a.m.	Drive to Cedar Key.
10:30 a.m.	Arrive at Cedar Key. See the museum.
11:30 a.m.	Wander Cedar Key's two-block waterfront. Watch the pelicans. Decide where to eat lunch.
12:00 noon	Lunch.
1:30 p.m.	Drive to Manatee Springs.
3:00 p.m.	Walk the boardwalk, hike the nature trail, swim or canoe.
Evening	Camp at Manatee Springs or check into a motel in Chiefland.

Travel Route: Ocala to Cedar Key (67 miles) to Manatee Springs (45 miles)
From Ocala, follow US 27 (Blichton Road, the northernmost of the three Ocala exits from Interstate 75) west for 21 miles to Williston, then US 27 Alt. for 12 miles west to Bronson. Turn south (left) on Highway 24. You will cross US 19/98 at Otter Creek after 11 miles. Stay on Highway 24 for 23 more miles to Cedar Key.

Leaving Cedar Key, retrace your route on Highway 24 to Otter Creek. Turn north (left) on US 19/98 and go 12 miles to Chiefland. Manatee Springs Road, on your left at the north end of town, runs about 7 miles west to the state park.

Sightseeing Highlights
▲▲ **Cedar Key**—There are no tourist attractions on Cedar Key (pop. 700). In fact, compared to almost anywhere else you've visited in Florida, it's downright dull. No rides, no beaches, no billboards, no resort hotels. Yet therein lies its charm. You see, a century ago Cedar Key was among the largest port cities in Florida, rivaling Tampa and Key West. The main reason was the Faber Company (the folks who originally decided that pencils should be yellow), which manufactured pencils here from Florida pine trees and graphite imported from Siberia.

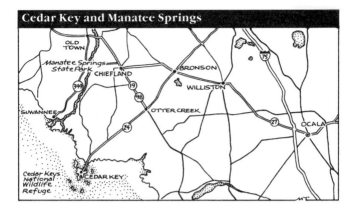

Cedar Key and Manatee Springs

Loads of pencils left here bound for all parts of the globe. Today, the pencil factory is gone and so are the ships and trains. The island, including residents' yards, is a national wildlife refuge. The modest **Cedar Key State Museum** (at the north end of the island, open Thursday through Monday from 9:00 a.m. to 5:00 p.m., closed Tuesdays and Wednesdays) recounts the boom era.

Cedar Key was the place where John Muir, the conservationist who later persuaded politicians to create Yosemite National Park in California and founded the Sierra Club, began his career. The 29-year-old freelance writer had undertaken a seven-week, thousand-mile walk from Indiana to the Gulf Coast to write a documentary account of social conditions in the post-Civil War South in 1867. On reaching Florida, he came down with malaria and stayed in Cedar Key during his recovery. While here, he first wrote down his philosophy that wilderness has value for its own sake.

Cedar Key's business district consists of a half-dozen seafood and short-order restaurants at the south end of the island. On the waterfront, you'll see lots of pelicans.

▲▲ **Manatee Springs State Park**—This large artesian spring, with a flow of 117 million gallons a day, is both a popular local swimming hole and a first-rate wildlife-viewing spot. As you stroll the boardwalk from the spring to the Suwannee River, notice the wading birds called limpkins dining on apple snails that live in the swamp. The park service goes out of its way to advise you that, despite the name, if you expect to see manatees here, you may be disappointed. However, we've spotted manatees grazing on the floating vegetation near the end of the boardwalk more often than anywhere else in Florida.

The spring run flows to the Suwannee River, the same one Stephen Foster immortalized in his song. If the Suwannee seems to bear little resemblance to the immortal lyrics, that's because

Foster never saw this river. He just liked the name. "S'wanee" was a big improvement on his original working title, "Way Down Upon the Peedee River."

In case you're wondering where all the water comes from which feeds springs like this one and Weeki Wachee, Homosassa, Silver, Juniper, and Salt springs, it seeps through the porous limestone that underlies most of the Florida peninsula and flows in underground rivers. Sometimes the roof collapses to form sinkholes. You can see several such sinkholes along the nature trail that starts just across from the campground in Manatee Springs State Park.

To rent a canoe and paddle up and down the spring run, see the man at the ramshackle general store just outside the park entrance. Manatee Springs State Park is open from 8:00 a.m. to sunset. Admission is $3 per vehicle.

Lodging

Northwest Florida is camping country, and the accommodations scene is generally bleak. In Chiefland, the **Cedar Oaks Motel** (904-493-2264) offers small rooms for under $30 a night. There are also the **Manatee Springs Motel** (under $35 a night, 904-493-2291) and the **Chiefland Motel** (904-493-1114).

Camping

Manatee Springs State Park is a beautiful place to camp, and the fee is only $6.

Another outstanding option is the **KOA Old Town/Suwannee River**. To get there, from Chiefland follow US 19 north for 14 miles and turn left on Highway 349, 2 miles to the campground following the yellow-and-red signs. The campground fronts on the Suwannee River and has a forested private nature preserve draped with Spanish moss. Whenever an alligator or manatee is sighted in the river, it's big news in the campground. Sites with full hookups including cable TV cost $17 a night.

WAKULLA SPRINGS

Wakulla Springs was once the private estate and nature preserve of the richest man in the state. Today, it belongs to the people of Florida. Enjoy it.

Suggested Schedule

9:00 a.m.	Drive to Wakulla Springs.
12:00 noon	Explore Wakulla Springs all afternoon.
3:30 p.m.	Campers, drive to Alligator Point. Noncampers, spend the night at Wakulla Springs Lodge.

Travel Route: Manatee Springs to Wakulla Springs (115 miles)

From Chiefland, take US 19/98 north to Perry, a distance of 67 miles.

Along this highway, a half-dozen roads lead west through pine timberlands to fishing camps and villages along Florida's "hidden coast." If you have plenty of extra time, take a long detour through little Steinhatchee and tiny Adams Beach by turning left onto County Road 358 about 12 miles north of Cross City, then right at Jena on County Road 361. The 48-mile trip will return you to the main highway a few miles south of Perry. There are no sightseeing highlights along this detour, but you'll feel like a real explorer as you discover a 100-mile stretch of the Florida coast that remains completely undeveloped and practically inaccessible. Beaches are small and far between, but bear in mind that 100 years ago Miami Beach too was covered with scrubby vegetation.

As you approach Perry on US 19/98, the Forest Capital State Museum is on your left near the southern edge of town.

Turn west (left) in Perry and follow US 98 for 38 miles to Newport. Turn right onto State Road 267 and follow it for 10 miles to Edward Ball Wakulla Springs State Park.

Sightseeing Highlights
▲ **Forest Capital State Museum**—Perry (pop. 8,500), the crossroads of one of the least inhabited parts of Florida, is the "capital" of the state's timber industry. In case you're interested in how paper and turpentine are made, you can find out in this little museum. Out back is a park with impressively big pine trees and a reconstructed nineteenth-century Cracker house.

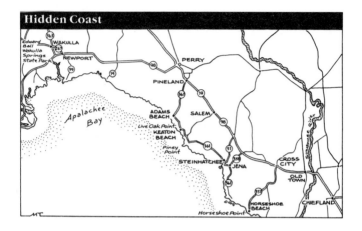

Hidden Coast

(Crackers were Floridian pioneers, named for the way they cracked their bullwhips to drive oxen. Native-born north Floridians today call themselves Crackers proudly.) Open from 9:00 a.m. to 5:00 p.m. daily, the museum charges a mere $.25 per person admission.

▲▲▲ **Edward Ball Wakulla Springs State Park**—The deepest artesian springs in Florida (185 feet), with an average flow of 600,000 gallons a day, Wakulla Springs forms a basin over an area of four-and-a-half acres with water so clear that you can actually see objects—including mastodon bones—on the bottom. Take the glass-bottom boat ride. There is also a "jungle" boat cruise that takes you downriver to see wildlife— birds, turtles, deer, and alligators—that lives protected by the 2,900-acre park. There are hiking and biking trails, too.

The park and lodge (see Lodging below) were the property of Edward Ball, a Florida politician who became the state's wealthiest financier with a little help from his in-laws, the DuPont family. The springs were acquired by the state of Florida in 1986 with help from the Nature Conservancy.

Wakulla Springs is open from 8:00 a.m. to sunset. Admission is $1 per vehicle and driver and $.50 per passenger. The glass-bottom boat and jungle cruises each cost $3.75 per adult, $2.25 per child ages 6 through 12; combination tickets for both cruises cost $6 per adult, $3.75 per child.

Lodging

There are only 27 guest rooms, so make your reservations well in advance—ideally, before you leave home—to stay at **Wakulla Springs Lodge**. Elegantly rustic, the 1937 lodge has Tennessee marble floors, Spanish archways and grillwork,

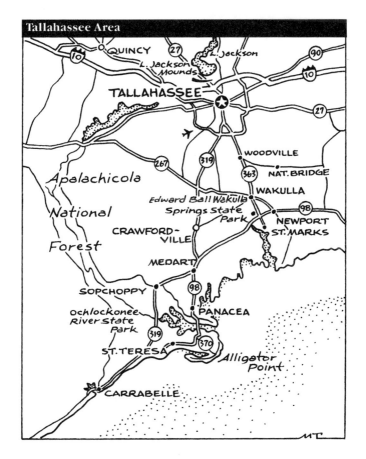

Tallahassee Area

Aztec-design ceiling beams, Old South period furnishings, and an incomparable setting in the heart of Wakulla Springs State Park. The lodge is operated by the Florida State University Center for Professional Development and Public Service, and rates are surprisingly low for quality accommodations, about $50 to $70 per night. The lodge dining room serves reasonably priced (under $12) dinners from 6:30 p.m. to 8:30 p.m. as well as breakfast and lunch. For further information and reservations, write Wakulla Springs Lodge, Wakulla Springs, FL 32305, or call (904) 224-5950. No pets.

Camping
There is no camping at Wakulla Springs. The nearest campground is the small one (13 sites) at **Newport Recreation**

Area, where US 98 crosses the St. Mark's River at Newport. The camping fee is $7.

A more secluded riverside campground is at **Ochlockonee River State Park**, 27 miles southwest of Newport. To get there, continue on US 98 to Medart, then turn west (right) on US 319; the park is on your left 5 miles south of Sopchoppy. Sites cost $15 a night with a $3 surcharge for out-of-staters.

A privately operated campground beside a long, beautiful, little-known beach is the **Alligator Point KOA**. To get there, from Newport stay on US 98 for 25 miles, passing through Medart and Panacea. Five miles south of Panacea, turn right on County Road 370 and follow the yellow-and-red KOA signs for another 5 miles. The camping fee is about $15 a night.

TALLAHASSEE

Tallahassee (pop. 112,000) is an "I can't believe I'm in Florida" city—dignified, peaceful, Deep Southern. The Capitol Center feels like a college campus swarming with lawyers instead of students, a world apart from the Florida you've explored in the past three weeks. In this ivory-towerish setting, lawmakers contemplate from a distance such problems as explosive growth, environmental crises, refugee invasions, and drug smuggling. You, too, might take a few minutes to look back on the many faces of Florida you've experienced during this trip.

Suggested Schedule

9:00 a.m.	Drive to Tallahassee.
10:00 a.m.	See the Florida history museum and the Old Capitol.
11:00 a.m.	Take the tour to the observation deck atop the new capitol.
12:00 noon	Picnic at Lake Jackson Mounds.
2:00 p.m.	Homeward bound on the interstate.

Travel Route: Wakulla Springs to Tallahassee (15 miles)
When you leave Wakulla Springs, continue west on State Road 267 for about 3 miles to US 319. (Coming north from Ochlockonee River State Park or Alligator Point, retrace your route and join US 319 at Medart.) Turn north (right) and drive 12 miles into the heart of downtown Tallahassee; the highway becomes Monroe Street and takes you directly to the capitol complex. Parking is at a premium around the capitol. Do not park in an unmetered space or you'll be towed away. Instead, continue three blocks past the capitol, turn right on East College Avenue, and go one block to the city parking garage on Calhoun Street. Walk back to the capitol from there.

Sightseeing Highlights
▲▲ **State Capitol Buildings**—Start with a self-guided tour of the Old Capitol, dwarfed by the modern high-rise capitol directly behind it and the House and Senate office buildings that flank it on both sides. The Old Capitol, used from 1902 to 1978, contains eight rooms of history exhibits on the second floor. It is open to the public Monday through Friday from 9:00 a.m. to 4:30 p.m., Saturdays from 10:00 a.m. to 4:30 p.m., and Sundays from 12:00 noon to 4:30 p.m. Free.

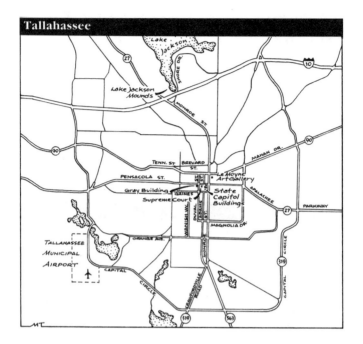

The present 22-story **capitol** has a top-floor observation deck that commands a bird's-eye view of Tallahassee, which appears as an island in a boundless ocean of trees. You can only visit the observation deck by taking a free tour, offered daily between the hours of 11:00 a.m. and 4:00 p.m.

The **Supreme Court** is located one block behind the capitol. The public can listen in on oral arguments and see the justices in action during the morning hours of the first week of each month.

▲▲**Museum of Florida History**—The museum, along with the state archives and state library, is in the R. A. Gray Building, two blocks west of the capitol building. Here you can see such varied exhibits of Floridiana as a mastodon, Spanish gold, a citrus packing house, and a tin can camper. The museum's History Shop may be your last chance for souvenirs of Florida—and it's a good one. The museum is open Monday through Friday from 9:00 a.m. to 4:30 p.m., Saturdays from 10:00 a.m. to 4:30 p.m., and Sundays from 12:00 noon to 4:30 p.m. Free.

▲**Historic Mansions**—From the municipal parking garage, follow one-way Gadsden Street north to the **LeMoyne Art Gallery** at 125 North Gadsden. This modest museum of local and regional art is in a lovely 1853 home, open Tuesday through Saturday from 10:00 a.m. to 5:00 p.m., Sundays 2:00 p.m. to 5:00 p.m. Free.

Another restored pre-Civil War mansion, the **Brokaw-McDougall House** at 329 North Meridian Street (one block east and two blocks north of the art gallery), is the headquarters of the Historic Tallahassee Preservation Board, open Monday through Friday from 8:00 a.m. to 5:00 p.m. They can provide information on dozens of other historic buildings around the city.

▲**San Luis de Talimani Archaeological Site**—Three miles west of the Capitol Center on US 90 (Mahan Drive), this site of a seventeenth-century Franciscan mission and Apalachee Indian village is still being excavated by the State Bureau of Archaeological Research. It is normally open to the public Monday through Friday from 9:00 a.m. to 4:30 p.m., Saturdays from 10:00 a.m. to 4:30 p.m., Sundays from 12:00 noon to 4:30 p.m. Check at the Museum of Florida History or call the museum (488-1484) or the site (487-3711) to find out when the archaeologists are at work. Free.

▲**Lake Jackson Mounds Recreation Area**—Follow Monroe Street (US 27) north past the interstate and watch for the turnoff on your right, then follow the signs to these two large pre-Columbian Mound Builders' pyramids. No artifacts are on display here, but the tops of the mounds and the park lawn surrounding them make for pleasant picnicking. A nature trail leads from the parking area past the ruins of an old sugar cane mill. The park is open daily from 8:00 a.m. to dusk. Free.

Back on the Interstate

Monroe Street will take you to Interstate 10 just north of town. If you're returning to the Atlantic coast, or if you started this itinerary in the middle and plan to continue to Day 1, it's a fast 176-mile, 3½-hour drive east to Jacksonville and Interstate 95.

If you're heading west, 200 miles (4 hours) can take you to the end of the panhandle and the Alabama state line. Or, if you have the time, retrace this morning's route and follow US 98 along the Gulf Coast. The 240-mile, all-day coastal route will take you through such diverse towns as Apalachicola (a quaint little oyster-fishing town where a small museum commemorates Dr. John Gorrie, who changed the course of Florida history by inventing air conditioning), Panama City (heart of what was formerly the "Redneck Riviera," a nickname only recently changed to the more dignified "Emerald Coast," of special interest to students of miniature golf architecture), and Fort Walton Beach (the current hot spot for name-brand resort hotel development). This route will take you along the Miracle Strip, a hundred miles of squeaky, sugar-white beach, and return you to the interstate at Pensacola.

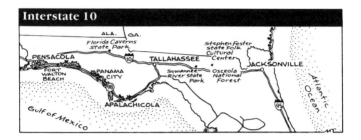

We hope you've enjoyed these Florida explorations as much as we've enjoyed bringing them to you. Before we say farewell, y'all, we'd like to point out that you can't leave Florida by car without driving through Dixie. Interstate 10 connects this book to its companion volume, *22 Days in Dixie* by Richard Polese, which guides independent travelers from New Orleans to Nashville to Savannah, including the Natchez Trace, Great Smokey Mountains National Park, the Blue Ridge Parkway, and numerous little-known pleasures and treasures in eight Deep South states.

INDEX

Other Books from John Muir Publications

Asia Through the Back Door, 3rd ed., Rick Steves and John Gottberg (65-48-3) 336 pp. $15.95

Being a Father: Family, Work, and Self, Mothering Magazine (65-69-6) 176 pp. $12.95

Buddhist America: Centers, Retreats, Practices, Don Morreale (28-94-X) 400 pp. $12.95

Bus Touring: Charter Vacations, U.S.A., Stuart Warren with Douglas Bloch (28-95-8) 168 pp. $9.95

Catholic America: Self-Renewal Centers and Retreats, Patricia Christian-Meyer (65-20-3) 325 pp. $13.95

Complete Guide to Bed & Breakfasts, Inns & Guesthouses, 1990-91 ed., Pamela Lanier (65-43-2) 504 pp. $15.95

Costa Rica: A Natural Destination, Ree Strange Sheck (65-51-3) 280 pp. $15.95

Elderhostels: The Students' Choice, Mildred Hyman (65-28-9) 224 pp. $12.95

Europe 101: History & Art for the Traveler, Rick Steves and Gene Openshaw (28-78-8) 372 pp. $12.95

Europe Through the Back Door, 9th ed., Rick Steves (65-42-4) 432 pp. $16.95

Floating Vacations: River, Lake, and Ocean Adventures, Michael White (65-32-7) 256 pp. $17.95

Gypsying After 40: A Guide to Adventure and Self-Discovery, Bob Harris (28-71-0) 264 pp. $12.95

The Heart of Jerusalem, Arlynn Nellhaus (28-79-6) 312 pp. $12.95

Indian America: A Traveler's Companion, Eagle/Walking Turtle (65-29-7) 424 pp. $16.95

Mona Winks: Self-Guided Tours of Europe's Top Museums, Rick Steves (28-85-0) 450 pp. $14.95

The On and Off the Road Cookbook, Carl Franz (28-27-3) 272 pp. $8.50

The People's Guide to Mexico, Carl Franz (28-99-0) 608 pp. $15.95

The People's Guide to RV Camping in Mexico, Carl Franz with Steve Rogers (28-91-5) 256 pp. $13.95

Preconception: A Woman's Guide to Preparing for Pregnancy and Parenthood, Brenda Aikey-Keller (65-44-0) 236 pp. $14.95

Ranch Vacations: The Complete Guide to Guest and Resort, Fly-Fishing, and Cross-Country Skiing Ranches, Eugene Kilgore (65-30-0) 392 pp. $18.95

Schooling at Home: Parents, Kids, and Learning, Mothering Magazine (65-52-1) $14.95

The Shopper's Guide to Mexico, Steve Rogers and Tina Rosa (28-90-7) 224 pp. $9.95

Ski Tech's Guide to Equipment, Skiwear, and Accessories, edited by Bill Tanler (65-45-9) 144 pp. $11.95

Ski Tech's Guide to Maintenance and Repair, edited by Bill Tanler (65-46-7) 144 pp. $11.95

A Traveler's Guide to Asian Culture, Kevin Chambers (65-14-9) 224 pp. $13.95

Traveler's Guide to Healing Centers and Retreats in North America, Martine Rudee and Jonathan Blease (65-15-7) 240 pp. $11.95

Undiscovered Islands of the Caribbean, Burl Willes (28-80-X) 216 pp. $12.95

Undiscovered Islands of the Mediterranean, Linda Lancione Moyer and Burl Willes (65-53-X) 184 pp. $13.95

22 Days Series

These pocket-size itineraries are a refreshing departure from ordinary guidebooks. Each author has an in-depth knowledge of the region covered and offers 22 tested daily itineraries through their favorite destinations. Included are not only ''must see'' attractions but also little-known villages and hidden ''jewels'' as well as valuable general information.

22 Days Around the World by R. Rapoport and B. Willes (65-31-9)
22 Days in Alaska by Pamela Lanier (28-68-0)
22 Days in the American Southwest by R. Harris (28-88-5)
22 Days in Asia by R. Rapoport and B. Willes (65-17-3)
22 Days in Australia, 3rd ed., by John Gottberg (65-40-8)
22 Days in California by Roger Rapoport (28-93-1)
22 Days in China by Gaylon Duke and Zenia Victor (28-72-9)

22 Days in Europe. 5th ed., by Rick Steves (65-63-7)
22 Days in Florida by Richard Harris (65-27-0)
22 Days in France by Rick Steves (65-07-6)
22 Days in Germany, Austria & Switzerland, 3rd ed., by Rick Steves (65-39-4)
22 Days in Great Britain, 3rd ed., by Rick Steves (65-38-6)
22 Days in Hawaii, 2nd ed., by Arnold Schuchter (65-50-5)
22 Days in India by Anurag Mathur (28-87-7)
22 Days in Japan by David Old (28-73-7)
22 Days in Mexico, 2nd ed., by S. Rogers and T. Rosa (65-41-6)
22 Days in New England by Anne Wright (28-96-6)
22 Days in New Zealand by Arnold Schuchter (28-86-9)
22 Days in Norway, Denmark & Sweden by R. Steves (28-83-4)
22 Days in the Pacific Northwest by R. Harris (28-97-4)
22 Days in Spain & Portugal, 3rd ed., by Rick Steves (65-06-8)
22 Days in the West Indies by C. & S. Morreale (28-74-5)

All 22 Days titles are 128 to 152 pages and $7.95 each, except *22 Days Around the World* and *22 Days in Europe*, which are 192 pages and $9.95.

''Kidding Around''
Travel Guides for Children

Written for kids eight years of age and older. Generously illustrated in two colors with imaginative characters and images. An adventure to read and a treasure to keep.

Kidding Around Atlanta, Anne Pedersen (65-35-1) 64 pp. $9.95
Kidding Around Boston, Helen Byers (65-36-X) 64 pp. $9.95
Kidding Around the Hawaiian Islands, Sarah Lovett (65-37-8) 64 pp. $9.95
Kidding Around London, Sarah Lovett (65-24-6) 64 pp. $9.95
Kidding Around Los Angeles, Judy Cash (65-34-3) 64 pp. $9.95
Kidding Around New York City, Sarah Lovett (65-33-5) 64 pp. $9.95
Kidding Around San Francisco, Rosemary Zibart (65-23-8) 64 pp. $9.95
Kidding Around Washington, D.C., Anne Pedersen (65-25-4) 64 pp. $9.95

Automotive Books

The Greaseless Guide to Car Care Confidence: Take the Terror Out of Talking to Your Mechanic, Mary Jackson (65-19-X) 224 pp. $14.95
How to Keep Your VW Alive (65-12-2) 424 pp. $19.95
How to Keep Your Subaru Alive (65-11-4) 480 pp. $19.95
How to Keep Your Toyota Pickup Alive (28-89-3) 392 pp. $19.95
How to Keep Your Datsun/ Nissan Alive (28-65-6) 544 pp. $19.95
Off-Road Emergency Repair & Survival, James Ristow (65-26-2) 160 pp. $9.95
Road & Track's Used Car Classics, edited by Peter Bohr (28-09-9) 272 pp. $12.95

Ordering Information
If you cannot find our books in your local bookstore, you can order directly from us. Your books will be sent to you via UPS (for U.S. destinations), and you will receive them approximately 10 days from the time that we receive your order. Include $2.75 for the first item ordered and $.50 for each additional item to cover shipping and handling costs. UPS will not deliver to a P.O. Box; please give us a street address. For airmail within the U.S., enclose $4.00 per book for shipping and handling. All foreign orders will be shipped surface rate; please enclose $3.00 for the first item and $1.00 for each additional item. Please inquire about foreign airmail rates.

Method of Payment
Your order may be paid by check, money order, or credit card. We cannot be responsible for cash sent through the mail. All payments must be made in U.S. dollars drawn on a U.S. bank. Canadian postal money orders in U.S. dollars are also acceptable. For VISA, MasterCard, or American Express orders, include your card number, expiration date, and your signature, or call (800)888-7504. Books ordered on American Express cards can be shipped only to the billing address of the cardholder. Sorry, no C.O.D.'s. Residents of sunny New Mexico, add 5.625% tax to the total.

Address all orders and inquiries to:
John Muir Publications
P.O. Box 613
Santa Fe, NM 87504
(800) 888-7504
(505) 988-1680 FAX